Setting up a library
and information service
from scratch

Setting up a library and information service from scratch

Sheila Pantry OBE and Peter Griffiths

facet publishing

Published by
Facet Publishing
7 Ridgmount Street
London WC1E 7AE

Facet Publishing (formerly Library Association Publishing) is wholly owned by
CILIP: the Chartered Institute of Library and Information Professionals.

First published 2005

British Library Cataloguing in Publication Data
A catalogue record for this book is available from the British Library.

ISBN 1-85604-558-7

Peter Griffiths writes in a personal capacity but is grateful for the Home
Office's agreement to the publication of his contribution to this book. Nothing
in this text should be taken as an official statement of policy, and mention of
any commercial service or product does not imply official endorsement.

Typeset in 11/14pt Aldine 401 and Verdana by Facet Publishing.
Printed and made in Great Britain by MPG Books Ltd, Bodmin, Cornwall.

Contents

Preface

There could be many reasons for establishing a library and information service; many organizations, especially small ones, get by without one and continue to survive or even to thrive nevertheless. But for sheer efficiency, continuity and up-to-date know-how it is cost effective for the majority of organizations, irrespective of background or subject area, to have organized collections of information with knowledgeable staff.

This book is intended as a basic guide to help those who need to set up a library and information service in their organization. It will help those who have qualifications but no experience in setting up such a centre, and guide those who have had no training at all.

The chapters take you step-by-step towards creating a successful service from scratch. We have drawn heavily on our experiences in setting up many information centres, not only in the UK, but also around the world, and we hope that you will enjoy the ideas we put forward and find them practical.

Chapter 1 looks at the reasons for establishing a library and information service, its role in the organization, what information *is*, and who needs this information; and shows that information is *not* all there on the internet free of charge. Authoritative and validated information sources are also discussed. Chapter 2 describes the first steps to be taken when setting up a library, who does what, what information is needed, and who needs it, and how to carry out an information audit.

Chapter 3 considers practical matters such as premises, furniture, equipment, internet access and other technical requirements. Staffing is a priority and requirements are outlined in Chapter 4, which includes sections on training and team-building. Chapter 5 describes information networks and ways of locating sources of information locally, nationally and internationally.

Chapter 6 looks at the variety of services to be provided by the information centre, including acquisitions, how to organize information, indexes and indexing, abstracts and abstracting, databases, enquiry services, reference collections and loan services, how to disseminate information, translation services and other services to particular user groups.

Various kinds of support for the library and information service are covered in Chapter 7, and Chapter 8 gives advice on how to promote it. Chapter 9 provides outlines for training various categories of potential users, and how to organize seminars and training courses.

Just in case you are new to the jargon of the information world, a glossary of useful terms is provided at the end of the book. This is followed by a reading list, which offers you further opportunities to delve into specific aspects of information work. The appendices provide some sample documents and support materials that may be useful.

We hope that you have as much enjoyment in setting up and running your information centre as we have had over the years and wish you every success in your work.

Sheila Pantry OBE
Peter Griffiths

1

Back to basics

●●●●●●●●●●●●●●●●●●●●●●●●●●●●●●●●●●●●●●●

In this chapter we look at:

- the reasons for establishing a library and information service
- whether information is all there on the internet and free
- what information is
- who needs information
- authoritative and validated information
- the roles of a library and information service.

●●●●●●●●●●●●●●●●●●●●●●●●●●●●●●●●●●●●●●●

Reasons for establishing a library and information service

Many organizations, especially small ones, get by without a library and continue to survive or even to thrive nevertheless. Communities such as societies and other non-commercial bodies often appear unable to afford to establish a library or the post of a qualified information specialist or librarian. So what is the reason why an information centre or library should be set up?

If you have been asked to set up a new centre then maybe that question has already been asked and answered under present circumstances. However, it would be as well to know the answer, or the answers, as sooner or later circumstances will change to the point where the existence of the service will be challenged, and that time is not the moment to go searching for the answers. If you are within an organization that is showing the signs of the need for an information service, then read on and see how much that service needs to be set up. Does your organization or community:

- hold many copies of the same information?
- spend money on acquiring it?
- lose it or discard it when it has been used once?
- spend money on acquiring it over and over?
- have staff who spend time trying to search for information without knowing if it is validated and authoritative?

It is all there on the internet and free isn't it?

Why would any organization want to set up its own information service? What advantages could there be in doing that? And what, therefore, does it think it wants you, as the information service provider or manager, to do what other members of the organization cannot do for themselves?

Information is after all widespread and pervasive. There is certainly more information in existence than at any time in history (by definition, when you think about it), but more than that it is increasing in quantity at a faster and faster rate. Estimates suggest it is doubling in little more than two years, and that people today can acquire more knowledge in a day than was known in a lifetime by people little more than a hundred years ago.

Along with the pervasiveness of information, the view seems to be increasing that managing this information and knowledge is a skill that takes no special ability or training, and that there is no problem in dealing with this mass of detail provided that this or that software is purchased and put to work on the organization's intranet. Not only this, the argument goes on, but there is at least one page on the internet where somebody has put all that anyone needs to know on any important subject, and that page is accurate, reliable, authoritative and timely – and available free of charge as the internet represents a kind of information-based virtual philanthropic institution. All such pages are flawlessly indexed by Google (for there is no other search engine), which can be relied on to place them at the top of the list of items retrieved no matter which term or synonym is entered. So it follows that there is no need for any information service in any organization or community, because now that internet access is universal all anyone needs to do is to navigate to Google and use the results to inform their business, social and educational decisions and opinions.

Somehow, we don't think so. The problem of course is that when the argument is set out like this an information professional recognizes at once how shallow and inaccurate it is – yet many people who are responsible for organizations or communities actually think like this. So you may have some work to do to convince the person or people who put you onto the creation of an information service that this is a serious job, and if that person is a convert then you may have to give them the evidence to contradict others who argue against having the information service.

The intention of this book is to do this by describing how to create and operate the kind of service that will meet the real information needs of its users, and provide a continuous reminder of the difference that library and information professionals make. In time you will acquire your own stock of stories and anecdotes that illustrate this value within your own community – for the time being you will have to rely on ours!

What is information?

We use information constantly and do not often stop to define it. Information is delivered in all kinds of containers. Libraries and information services have long collected a wide range of materials, typically books and journals, but more recently they have started to collect audiovisual materials and electronic materials. Have you considered every format that your customers may want to use? Identify them and compare with our list below, which includes just some of the ways that information can be stored. Recently the focus is not so much on collection as it is on access – so that it is not always necessary for the information service to own a physical copy of every item that its users want, but for the staff to know where and how to obtain it.

Often therefore the important thing is to know not what a customer has asked for but what information he or she is seeking. This can mean enquiring what the person is trying to achieve in order to identify the information that they need rather then want, and then in turn the source of the answers. The information could be factual, or the enquirer could be seeking a range of opinions or interpretations of a subject to support their studies. In other words, while there could be a single factual answer to an enquiry (for example, 'The sun sets tonight at 9.30 p.m.') there could also be a range of answers ('The causes of World War 2 were . . . ') and those answers could be controversial. This view of information counters the proposal given above that all necessary information can now be found through internet search engines without the need for a library or for an information professional.

There are numerous information sources, including:

- books, reports, pamphlets, etc. (one-off, print on paper)
- journals, newsletters (print on paper, serial)
- newspapers
- computer databases (full text, bibliographic, statistical)
- electronic journals and electronic books
- legislation (primary, secondary)
- guidance, codes of practice, official circulars
- research results (not necessarily collated or published)
- films, videos, DVDs
- press releases
- standard specifications
- advice
- encyclopedias, handbooks
- datasheets
- translations
- microfiche and microfilm
- CD-ROMs and DVD-ROMs
- computer disks (hard and floppy)
- software
- organizations (commercial, government, associations, federations, trade bodies, etc.)
- training materials.

Who needs information?

The clients of an information service may be closely defined, for example if the service is provided for a company or for the members of an organization. On the other hand you may find that the customers can be anyone from anywhere, as with a public library or enquiry service. Although you might be able to say that the primary customer group of public services will be drawn from people who live in the locality, they are open to all and you may find yourself dealing with telephone callers and e-mail correspondents who are far removed from where you are but have an interest in your local history or have a family connection that they want to trace.

Authoritative and validated information

Although many people and organizations seem to be convinced that all the answers they need are there online and can be accessed using Google, it is remarkable how easily they will accept the results of a search without questioning the authority or the validity of the information that they retrieve. There are many reports of people caught out by the convincing but bogus websites that have been built by fraudsters trying to obtain banking details from individuals and corporate bodies. Alongside the websites of many organizations there are spoof versions that are designed to mislead and discredit the genuine bodies. Sites are created that give inaccurate or biased information in order to dissuade customers or to do financial harm to their targets.

Information can often be inadvertently misquoted. Do you work in a specialist area where it needs an informed eye to recognize an error? Would your customers check the results of a web search before they used them – maybe with measurements quoted in the wrong units or a misplaced decimal point? Would they look for corroboration before passing the information or basing a business decision on the information? If you cannot answer yes to all these questions then you need to tell people about the value of a professional information service!

Authoritative information

Figure 1.1 shows what are apparently two websites for the World Trade Organization – but which one is genuine: **www.wto.org** or **www.gatt.org**? It is now easier to tell them apart than it used to be because one is updated more frequently than the other, but it would be easy for the unwary to confuse the two. One is in fact a rogue website designed to discredit the WTO, but it draws heavily on the design and the graphics of the genuine website.

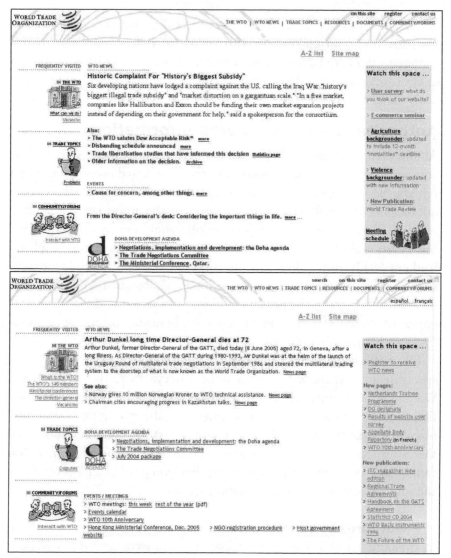

Figure 1.1 Which website is genuine?

Even the best journalists can be fooled. In December 2004 the BBC website ran a story to mark the twentieth anniversary of the Bhopal disaster based on an interview with a 'spokesman' for the Dow Chemical company who said that the corporation had admitted liability and set up a compensation fund. In fact the story was entirely spurious and could be traced back to an organization known as the Yes Men. The problem appeared to be that the

interview request had been sent to an e-mail address linked to the
website **www.dowethics.com**. A check of the registration data
would have shown this not to be owned by Dow Chemical or the
Union Carbide company that previously owned the Bhopal factory,
but by an activist located in Bhopal. The language of the website
should also have set warning bells ringing among the journalists
covering the story.

Griffiths (2001) describes other case studies showing the possibili-
ties for error if information is used without corroboration.

These examples show the importance of using validated and authoritative
information. If you need to convince your organization of the need for an
information service, provide evidence that relying on the internet and on
search engines alone can be inadequate and sometimes downright dangerous.

The roles of an information service

Whether they are serving a community (such as a local area, a school or
college), a commercial or public organization, or an academic community,
information services are an essential element of that community. Library
and information professionals carry out a wide range of activities apart
from simply providing an enquiry service or a lending service. Information services also provide electronic information services to their users;
they identify and purchase publications for their clients, and they create
and manage websites and intranets. Information services provide their
users with regular information updates on topics of interest, or monitor
websites and publications for mentions of the organization or community
that they serve.

Library and information professionals analyse and sift information and
compile publications that inform their clients by keeping them in touch
with developments in their community, or academic subject, or areas of
interest. They record information so that it can be retrieved, through cataloguing, indexing, abstracting and database building. They provide links
to the information either by organizing the collection using classification
schemes that link to the information centre's catalogue, or by hyperlink-
ing to internet resources. Not least, if they don't have the answer they find

out what it is, or put their customer in touch with the expert. In short, they provide their communities with a range of unique services that put information at the centre of the community's activities.

Summary

We have seen that:

- Many organizations waste money and time by obtaining multiple copies of the same information.
- There are many sources of information, but not all of them can be trusted.
- Information certainly isn't all free and on the internet.
- Library and information professionals have a special role to play, putting users in touch with information and providing a range of services to support that role.
- The skills of library and information professionals are needed in many organizations, and the information centres they create are a valuable resource.

2

The first steps

● ●

In this chapter we look at:

- The need for your library and information service
- Establishing requirements with information audits
- Convincing the undecided
- Outcome of your information audit
- Using professional skills in a wider context
- Building customer loyalty
- Communication and the information audit
- Next steps.

● ●

Information services should be central to every organization irrespective of the field of activity (or 'sector' – whether academic, government, workplace, public, legal, financial, technical, scientific or medical). At some time in the lifetime of all information services questions should be asked about their role, function, effectiveness and cost benefit to their users; it is especially useful to do this at the outset when setting up a new library or information centre. It is also important to consider these matters when building electronic services for a sometimes unseen audience.

Reviewing the need for work

An initial review before starting a service will ask a number of key questions about the service and its future business plan. It will look at existing systems and their quality, and at the proposals for a new system or for improvements to what currently exists. This review will need to be frank if not brutal in its appraisal of the services and systems and must strive to deliver improvements to users. Our approach is based on information auditing, and insists on considered responses to questions like these:

- What is the core business of the information service?
- How is it doing?
- Why are particular jobs in the service done, need they be continued, and can the need for any of them be avoided?
- How are jobs done, why are they done in a particular way, and can a better way be found?
- When jobs are done, why then? Can a better time be found?
- Where are jobs done, why there? Can a better place be found?
- Who does this job? Why is it done by them/him/her? Is there someone else inside the organization or outside, who can do this job?
- Are the staff able to deliver the services or products – what training will be needed?

Where the question has been asked with the word 'can?' ask it again with the word 'should?' This will open up two further issues for decision, depending on the answer to the question containing the word 'can?' If the answer was 'no', is it worth investigating to find out whether a way can be found to do things better, and if the answer was 'yes', does it follow that the service should go to some alternative supplier or that some other means should be found of providing the service? The process is likely to be uncomfortable, as the assumed answer until now has usually been 'everything's fine, thanks'. In the present climate, you will have to show that not only is all truly excellent, but that you have looked at other ways of doing things excellently and made a balanced decision that your way is better.

The role of customers

In order to achieve the quality of service and the performance targets you will have to make your customers aware that they too have a role to play. Customers should:

- be aware of what the information service can do
- identify their information needs

- agree to take those needs to the information service as first port of call
- communicate them to the information service staff and discuss them as required
- give feedback to the information service
- keep information service staff aware of their changing subject interests
- involve the information service in projects that have information implications.

Ultimately it is the customer who decides the quality of the services, by:

- making demands for improvements on an existing service
- asking for new services
- showing a willingness to co-operate.

Helping the customer to describe information needs

The customer may need help in order to be able to contribute. The tool by which this is done is an information audit, which has equal potential in public service and in academic environments as in the workplace library services where it was first developed. It is an important and valuable technique that yields data about the information resources held within the organization or community, its match to the information requirements of the customer group, and the opportunities for intrapreneurial behaviour. In creating a successful library or service the library and information service (LIS) manager will need to carry out an information audit that makes people stand back and analyse the 'why', 'how', 'where' and 'what' exactly the information service should be trying to achieve. There will be ample opportunities to develop services once this knowledge is acquired.

Organizational needs

An important task for information managers is to get a clear understanding of the entire organization or community in which the service will operate. Without this understanding the library and information service will not achieve a central role in the user community. A LIS that is driven by a vision shared only by its own staff will never be seen as important by the community or organization that it serves.

Irrespective of the subject background, the organization's or the client's needs should be identified and captured before work begins on any alteration to the service, or the identification of the electronic components within it. The first step is to carry out an information audit of the organization's information needs. It should aim to discover not only what information is being created or brought into the organization, but it should also aim to discover the purpose to which information is being put in case this reveals more effective alternative sources.

Information audits

The basic function of information audits is to assess a community's or an organization's information needs, to identify what it already holds, and to report on the gap between the two as a basis for action.

Information audits can be developed from this basic assessment to provide a wealth of important data such as:

- what information exists within the organization or community
- where it is located
- where it is obtained from (or where it is created)
- how many sections within the organization or the community being served have their own collections of information, and which of these have an official branch of the information service
- what information the organization needs and when it is needed
- who uses it
- what gaps exist
- where potential customers for information are located
- why people use a particular service or source of information in preference to others
- why some people use the service frequently, some occasionally and some never
- what formats the information is required in
- what training is needed for both staff and users.

Armed with this data, the LIS manager can begin to put together the range of services that will meet the needs of the greatest number of users in the most cost-effective way. But remember that it can take considerable time from initial consultation and information audit to the final outcomes in the form of new or revised services. For example, a consultation exercise carried out at the UK Royal College of Nursing took a full two years to complete (Hyams, 2001).

To obtain the data, the LIS manager should survey managers or other representatives (depending on the type of community being served) to gather details of the types of information that members of that community need. This can be done by questionnaires and structured interviews; less controlled methods can be used such as sending feedback cards with library transactions but the results will probably be less reliable. The exercise should provide a clear understanding of the ways that users currently access information, and of the types of information that they use.

As well as revealing what kind of information is needed, who needs it, and the range of topics that must be covered, an information audit will also show requirements for any kind of information that is not currently available in the organization. It will help to identify any regular specialist information needs together with systems and services being used to meet those requirements. You will often find that people are using external sources such as their professional society or even the local public library because it does not occur to them to ask their own information specialists.

Information audits frequently uncover the same kind of poor information use that highlight the need for an information service. They often find that people:

- treat information as power – but may fail to tell anyone else what information they hold
- keep information in databases that run on old software, which makes the databases difficult to maintain and the information difficult to share
- keep old information and use it as if it were current – which is dangerous
- get information from sources outside the organization or outside the community but don't check whether it is valid – especially if they have paid for it
- use incompatible systems, e.g. e-mail software can erase attachments when it sends them to another network
- think they know how to use information resources, but actually they don't, which leads to poor use of expensive resources
- duplicate work, duplicate purchases of information, and duplicate the invention of the wheel, because they don't share and they don't ask before they buy.

We believe that these problems can be identified and eliminated using the information audit techniques that we cover in more detail in a number of our books. You will find sections on information audit in different contexts in *Creating a Successful E-information Service* (Pantry and Griffiths, 2002), *Developing a Successful Service Plan* (Pantry and Griffiths, 2000), *Becoming a Successful Intrapreneur* (Pantry and Griffiths, 1998) and *Managing Outsourcing in Library and Information Services* (Pantry and Griffiths, 2004). Details of these books and of some helpful articles are included in the references.

Typical questions and activities that are used in information audits include:

- Which information resources do you believe support the organization's aims and objectives and its programme of work (or the community's activities, or whatever is a relevant version of this question)?
- Can you categorize these information sources into the following groups: essential, desirable, nice to have?
- Where (in which departments or with which people) does the information reside?
- How up to date is it, and how is it maintained (both with regard to its contents and to ensuring that all copies are the same)?
- Where are the gaps in existing information flows and currently held information?
- As well as these gaps, what other major information needs exist?
- How many different computer-based information systems are in use already?
- How many people in the community use externally based information services already, e.g. online databases, the internet, CD-ROMs?
- Are all community members fully trained and able to use the computerized services and technologies?
- If not, how much training is needed, and at what level?
- Finally, ask individuals: 'On what information do you depend to carry out your job (or any regular activity in the community)?'

These questions and your discussions may well uncover poor information management habits like the ones mentioned above. Your task as the manager of the library or information centre is to introduce awareness and training programmes that tackle and eliminate these habits by showing the members of your community how to use your valuable resources. You will find a growing body of helpful advice on this subject under the heading 'information literacy'.

Defining information resources and services

In our recently revised book, *The Complete Guide to Preparing and Implementing Service Level Agreements* (Pantry and Griffiths, 2001), we urged the use of a glossary or other agreed list of definitions to avoid any question of ambiguity over the questions asked in the audit and the interpretation.

We have found considerable evidence that many managers understand neither the issues that information professionals have to deal with in purchasing and managing information, nor the terminology we use to describe those activities. Many terms have multiple definitions and multiple meanings that need to be defined. For example: do we speak of routing or circulation for journals?; or does circulation involve journals (or periodicals . . .) or books (or monographs . . .)?; and when I say 'urgent' is that what you call 'rush'?; and so on. Now bear in mind that many of the staff who let contracts do not properly understand what any of the terms mean, whichever alternative is right, and you will see the potential for chaos.

As information professionals we often seek the endorsement of other managers for our activities, but they do not understand the consequences of what we seek to do. Imagine the situation reversed: would you sanction a major re-organization of a financial or legal service if you had no idea what the service was providing because the description was ambiguous or meaningless, or couched in financial jargon you did not understand? Would your answer be the same if it was a service you did not personally use?

Arguments to convince the undecided

So, an information audit seeks to answer a number of questions about information and its use in the organization. Some of these questions should convince management (or the people funding the service) of the value of time and effort spent on the information audit activity. And as we just saw, it will highlight those areas where poor use is being made of costly resources.

But what if you need to convince management that an information audit, which can be costly in time and effort, is needed? The key questions below address the most disruptive of the poor information habits that we have been looking at. Are there positive answers to all these questions? There should be if the decision is to do without an information audit.

- Are you certain that there is effective control of information resources and the organization's (or the community's) expenditure on them?
- Can you say what the customers' main information needs are and whether they are satisfied?
- How many different computer based information systems exist already and what information do they contain? Is the information reliable and compatible? Would they all provide the same accurate answer to a given question? What do your major customers already use as information services? Do they provide reliable information? Are you holding different answers to those questions?
- How many staff use external based information services already, e.g. online databases, the internet, CD-ROMs? Are these better than internal sources? What external information services do you – and your customers – have access to? Do you have, or need, a budget to access or buy information?
- Are all users fully trained and able to use the computerized services and technologies?

Outcomes

By carrying out an information audit you will be able to:

- know how the library and information service and its products are perceived – or not!
- determine and describe the organization's real information needs
- find out where the library and information service's customers are in the organization
- understand why people in the organization go elsewhere for information
- identify who really needs information
- know how to provide the information when it is needed
- understand the importance of producing information in the format customers need
- use the results of the information audit in any future publicity.

Once the information audit has been completed then the rethinking and discussion about any outsourcing of the service(s) can go ahead in the knowledge that the information services will be providing the services the customers need and want. The added bonus is that the knowledge that the information centre staff gain about the organization from doing the audit will increase their standing in the community.

Wider use of information professional skills: reputation management

We are aware of a number of new fields of work for information professionals, and believe these may help to influence people deciding whether to agree to a new or improved library or information centre. An example of one of these new fields is reputation management, which is a term that covers two ideas, both of which relate to skills that librarians typically demonstrate. One of these ideas is ensuring that the quality and reputation of the services within the organization remains at the highest possible level, while the other idea is looking after the good name of the organization and its services in the public arena. Branding and quality management are important elements of the first activity, while the second extends into the area sometimes known as 'competitive intelligence' or even 'information warfare'.

So far as the information centre manager is concerned, it will be important to provide a service to the user community of the highest possible standard, one that will support the organization in maintaining its reputation and where the flow of high quality information could be one of the things that the reputation is founded upon.

The internet usability expert Jakob Nielsen is credited with the first widely accepted definition of reputation management. In his original definition the reputation manager was someone whose job was to co-ordinate large numbers of quality judgements provided by users of a service. By 1999 Nielsen had refined his definition of reputation management as follows:

> an independent service that keeps track of the rated quality, credibility, or some other desirable metric for each element in a set. The things being rated will typically be websites, companies, products, or people, but in theory anything can have a reputation that users may want to look up before

taking action or doing business. The reputation metrics are typically collected from other users who have had dealings with the thing that is being rated. Each user would indicate whether he or she was satisfied or dissatisfied. In the simplest case, the reputation of something is the average rating received from all users who have interacted with it in the past.

(Nielsen, 1999)

Information professionals were involved in the beginning of the discipline of reputation management; their skills will help to maintain their reputation within your organization and your organization's reputation in the market place. But there is a further way of using the information professional's skills, which is to monitor your reputation, sharing what is found and ensuring that action is taken to remedy any untrue statements. This monitoring activity is very important in commercial circles but the technique can be applied to any sort of organization. You could just buy in press cuttings that mention your community or organization, but there is a wealth of information and comment on the internet that needs to be monitored, and new software has become available that allows you to build profiles and monitor positive and negative presentations of your reputation. Most recently, the phenomenon of 'blogging' – the writing of weblogs, which are like electronic diaries kept up to date on websites – has lent a new urgency to this area of work. Where employees can easily publish their thoughts (and your secrets!) to the whole world, and where both well-wishers and those who would do you harm have equal access to instant communication, this is an area that few can now ignore!

Users take account of both the organization's reputation and that of its information service in deciding, for example, whether to use information from the web without further corroboration, and services that collaborate with your information service take reputation partly into account when deciding the degree to which they will work in co-operation with you.

The area of reputation management is still developing rapidly but provides a good example of the ways that information professional skill can be applied to a range of jobs. Think laterally and evaluate any areas that look as if they may be worthwhile investing time and money in.

Building customer loyalty and keeping it

Experience of building information services and electronic products, and of retaining customers over many years, has given us an insight into the behaviour of customers. They:

- like to be consulted before, during and after the service or product is available
- like customer care in all its aspects: e-mails, telephone calls, focus groups, etc.
- will tell others about you – see our comments above about managing the reputation of your service, and how it affects the overall reputation of your community
- will let you know what the competition is doing, and how well
- will tell you what is new that should be included in your electronic product
- like to have contact with a staff member they know – think about the way account managers operate in public relations or personnel
- do not like changes without consultation – so make sure that your communications are excellent!

Communication and the information audit

As we have just indicated, communication is an essential part of an information audit. People need to know what is going on, why it is happening and what is likely to happen afterwards. When the benefits start to be felt, people should be told what has been achieved and left in no doubt that this is down to the work done by the library and information service. There need to be positive incentives for people to switch to your new ways of doing things, and one good way of doing this is to tell them about the successes that they could be part of.

What new items of information has your work created? These could be:

- descriptive documents setting out the way information is managed in the community
- statements of information requirements around the organization, which could be shared with those just starting to define what they want
- statements saying what is available within the organization, but including any notes about restrictions because of security, licences or other factors

- an analysis of the difference between the above two sets of statements – a gap analysis
- recommendations on providing further information services or on changes in information technology management that could assist information users
- the business cases used to justify access to information services.

Sharing these will help other information users (actual or potential) as well as demonstrating to the key decision-makers in your user community that the information service means business.

Your full information audit report is likely to be too long for many of your senior users to have time or inclination to read. Summarize it to bring out the salient points. Don't just make this a short report – two pages of A4 should be your limit – but create a presentation as well. Your intranet is a good channel for making this available to everyone and you can send e-mails to your key decision-makers containing a link to the report. If you are working in a non-corporate environment so there is no intranet, consider putting this information onto an internet website.

Endorsement by your senior users will make your audit even more effective so make sure that they see it and tell you that they support it.

What next?

The answer to this final question is simple: get ready to do it again. Information needs and information resources both develop constantly, so what was a good match can become less good. Go to see your heaviest users at regular intervals and others as often as you can manage. Use the questionnaires as a basis to see what has altered and what has remained the same – and adjust your services accordingly.

Summary

It is essential to look closely at the organization's information needs and consult all the stakeholders before any work is carried out establishing a service. The information audit and subsequent consultancy may well provide some surprises but hopefully it will verify the need for good quality information services that satisfy the customers' needs.

3

Establishing the library and information service

● ●

In this chapter we look at:

- what kind of premises suit a library and information service
- how to ensure good design for your centre
- what makes a good or bad location
- what kind of furniture you will need
- how lighting and signage should be arranged
- what kind of equipment is needed
- what security issues you need to think about
- how to ensure you have good acoustics in your centre
- what access issues you must address – often by law
- how to make sure your effort in all this is maintained.

● ●

Once you have made the decision to establish an information centre and have found the information requirements of users, you can get on with the business of setting up the centre itself. This is a complex task, and you will need to devote a considerable time to assembling the furniture and equipment that will be required as well as finding a suitable location for the service. Do not be tempted to underestimate the time taken, for example by agreeing to an opening date that is unrealistic. If you are the only person who will be doing the work to set up the service, allow for the fact

that you will need to do other things with some of your time (not least, you may decide that you are due for a holiday).

Premises

An information centre does not necessarily need a large physical space, especially if it is starting from scratch in the 21st century. Electronic services will provide you with much of what you and your customers will need, but you will need adequate space for the computers and printers that will give access to the services. If your information centre is being set up because there is a need to store collections of documents (for example, internal reports if you operate within a company or a charity) then you will need space to store those documents and for some expansion. And whatever kind of centre you are running, you will need space for printed items for the foreseeable future; like the paperless office, the paperless library is still a long way off.

Information centres have to operate in all kinds of locations and environments but you should try to avoid as many problems as possible. Identify the ideal location for the service and negotiate from there. Often the people who make decisions about the physical location of the centre are genuinely unaware of the good and bad aspects of a location, so share your knowledge of operating a service.

Remember that you and your customers will need to occupy some of the space in your information centre. How many staff will it need to run the service? Are they 'front line' or 'back room' staff? Does it matter if they are doing back room tasks in front line space? In a small centre there may be no choice about it, and the staff will need to be accessible to the customers no matter what they are doing. In larger libraries, customers may expect to deal with dedicated enquiry staff, so space is needed where other tasks can be done out of sight or at least without inconveniencing the users of the information centre. Similarly, ask yourself how many users you expect to be in the centre at a time. Will they need somewhere to sit with the materials you locate for them, or must they take them away to their place of work or to their homes? How many people do you expect to be in the centre at one time? You need to address all of these questions because the answers will tell you how much space you need to leave for staff and customers.

We shall return more than once to the issue of health and safety, and to the access requirements of disability discrimination legislation. Do not plan problems into your designs! Make sure that you leave adequate clearances between items of furniture and between hard construction. Look at the design from a user's point of view and ensure that it meets the requirements.

Design

Within the space that you are allocated, you need to get these elements into a welcoming design that allows you to manage your stock, your staff and your customers. The design should be as open as space constraints allow, so that you can manage the activities in your library as effectively and simply as possible. If young people use the service, ensure they can be observed both for their own safety and that of other users. Make sure space for noisy or hectic activities does not impinge more than absolutely necessary on study areas. Provide the staff with secure accommodation for their possessions in what is after all an attractive public space, and ensure their personal security if that is any particular concern, for instance in an isolated building. Consider whether you need help in setting out a design. You will need to get your own ideas checked to ensure that they do not infringe health and safety or disability discriminations requirements, but a more complex design in a large area may benefit from the eye of a professional architect or designer. There is a growing body of information on library design that you, as the library and information professional, can draw on to support your designer or architect.

Contrasts between good and poor locations

Table 3.1 overleaf shows some contrasts between good and poor locations. In practice you will be very lucky to obtain all the 'good' elements and unlucky to be stuck with all the 'poor' elements.

Before you commit your ideas to a design, ask what activities will take place in the information centre. Is it just going to be a place where documents are stored and retrieved, or will it be more? You will almost certainly need space for your information and communications technology (ICT) but what else? Will there be regular meetings and gatherings? Do you want people to have space to sit and read either at tables or in more informal surroundings? (Either of these will have an effect on your need for lighting.) Do you intend to have an area where people can exchange ideas and information, or alternatively do you want to designate a quiet area because the norm in your service will be for people to talk and discuss matters? If your service will have children as a major customer group, does your design also need to allow for other customers to have separate and perhaps calmer areas for their needs?

Table 3.1 Good and poor locations for an information centre

Good location	Poor location
Position that members of the organization or community pass frequently	Remote location, not visible to members of the community or organization, not somewhere they go
Well lit and open	Dark, dingy, cramped
Visible, e.g. well signposted, with glass walls	Invisible, e.g. one door in blank wall, no signs or advertisements
Near other communal areas, e.g. eating and drinking facilities	Away from areas where people congregate, especially if people are expected to be seen at work constantly
Central location, such as near an entrance, lifts or stairs, and not at one extreme or other of a tall building	Remote from circulating areas, or isolated in the basement or at the top of the building
Safe from possible water damage	Near to pipes, glass roofs or other sources of damage
Well ventilated and heated	Stuffy, damp or liable to become dusty (or prone to weather extremes)
Well lit	Poorly lit – either too dark or in direct sunlight all the time
Adequate space for the service (including people, stock and equipment)	Not enough room for staff and stock; no room for IT equipment; many separate rooms instead of one space with some subdivisions; lots of stock in dispersed storerooms
Near key users	A long way from your key users (who are also your supporters)

Inside the building

Furniture

Library and information centre furniture must be chosen carefully if you and your customers are to get the best out of your premises. You could function well enough with some bookshelves, tables and chairs chosen from a general catalogue but these are not going to be as well suited to running an information service as specialist furniture would be.

Bookshelves will need to be adjustable to the size of publications, so you might find you need shelving capable of taking A4-sized documents (and therefore needing shelves spaced at around 33–35 cm, and capable of supporting a substantial weight without the shelf bending or the supports falling out). Beware designs that assume that every book is the size of a standard hardback novel and only provide shelving capacity based on that assumption.

Desks must provide users with some room to spread out but also with sufficient privacy to work without disturbance (and in some information centres it will be important for them to have privacy to research without being overlooked). Seats will have to be comfortable enough for your users to work for some hours if necessary without fatigue or backache. Think health and safety and take notice of the guidance and advice published by various authoritative organizations around the world, such as the UK Health and Safety Executive (HSE), US National Institute for Occupational Safety and Health (NIOSH), and the European Agency for Safety and Health at Work. See the references for links to useful websites.

Lighting

Many activities in a library, not least reading, should take place in well-lit conditions. Others activities are less light dependent, and over-bright lighting or reflections can cause difficulties in reading information from computer and television screens. General standards for office lighting should meet many needs, but again seek guidance and advice from organizations that produced publications such as standards organizations in most countries, the Chartered Institution of Building Services Engineers (CIBSE) *Code for Interior Lighting* and the linked Society of Light and Lighting publications. You need to note also the legal requirements for emergency lighting.

Signage

Is it obvious that you are running an information centre? Probably not as obvious as you think, which is why you need proper signage. Proper, professionally made signs will tell your patrons where you are, give them other essential information, like when they can get in, and help them find their way around once they are inside. Make sure that there is a sign at the entrance of the building telling people where they can find the information centre or library.

Sometimes there are problems (such as when a building has a preservation order on it and signs cannot be erected) but there is a world of difference between poorly made amateur signs – which give an unprofessional image – and well-made signs, especially those provided by sign makers rather than run off using a range of type faces on a laser printer. Just because you can print out a notice on a sheet of pink A4 paper and attach it to a window with sticky tape doesn't mean you should do it!

The public library on the Roelof Hartplein

On the Roelof Hartplein in Amsterdam is a notable public library building that forms a major element of this architecturally important square. The façade is symmetrical and has two large entrance doors, one on either side of the library windows, one leading to the library and the other to the flats built above it. Signage is fairly non-existent (apart from the words Openbaar Bibliotheek in large letters at high level above the street) so that it is difficult to tell how to get into the library. The best clue is on the door that leads to the flats, where a handwritten note announces in several languages that this is not the library! Maybe it's difficult to work responsibly with a building of high architectural significance or interest, but it doesn't have to be as difficult as this.

Equipment, internet access and consumables

Specifying your technical requirements can be a complex matter. Much library equipment is specialist in its construction and use, particularly if your organization still holds information in little used or obsolete formats such as microcard. (You could be a lot better off by having information converted to a current digital format.) Apart from furniture and IT equipment, you are likely to need specialist items to label, issue and return publications; to record and store details of your patrons if these are not held on computer; to maintain and repair your stock; and to work on new stock and do a million other jobs that are necessary in the information service.

Photocopiers, printers and facsimile (fax) machines

You will also need to think about a photocopier and any charging policy. This also has implications for your budget because you will need to think about the financing of consumables such as paper and toners, not to mention any maintenance charges. This is also applicable to printers. Likewise if you decide that a separate fax machine is necessary you will need paper for it. More and more information is transferred via the computer but the fax machine may still have a role to play.

Microfiche reader/printer

It may be necessary to have some sort of microfiche reader available, depending upon the type of information you wish to hold. Using a reader/printer the required information on microfiche may be selected, enlarged to enable it to be read, and paper copies printed if required.

Audiovisual equipment

Depending upon the requirements of users it may be necessary to have audiovisual equipment available; for example, if there is a large number of films, videos, collections of slides and transparencies produced for training purposes. In order to use this type of material an information centre needs the appropriate equipment; for example an overhead projector, slide projector, television and a video or DVD player.

Internet

You may have to comply with your organization's rules on access to the internet, which may give you some challenges to resolve before you can provide services to your customers – especially if you intend to use the organization's internet connection rather than access it via a direct external connection.

Consumables

Your organization may have a central supply for stationery; if not, you need to think about financing your letter-headed stationery, compliment slips, envelopes, jiffy bags and printed brochures. These items can consume a large percentage of the budget, so it is worth keeping control of expenditure.

Postage

Who pays for any postage? Again you need to make sure if the organization funds this centrally or whether you have to budget for it.

Security

How secure is the equipment and stock in your information centre? It has value to an opportunist thief as well as to someone more determined to separate you from the contents of your library. Some obvious measures include locking the centre outside your business hours, or perhaps making it clear that anyone who has the key for out of hours access must share the responsibility for security. IT equipment can be secured by using metal cables and heavy-duty fixings on the desk and the computer (versions for portable equipment feature padlocks so that you can release the computer if you need to do so). Publications are often intended to be taken out of the information centre (in most cases) but if pilfering is a problem then security tags can be inserted fairly cheaply into your stock. These are then kept live while the stock is in the library and deactivated when they are issued to a customer. A detector at the door should identify items that are being borrowed without permission. You will probably keep particularly valuable stock in a locked cupboard with very few keys (the cupboard could have a glass front to allow users to see what is in it).

So much for physical security. What about staff security? In some libraries, such as those in prisons, special features are built in to provide instant help if staff have problems; do you need a similar facility in a library situated in an isolated or otherwise vulnerable location? Consider the position and take appropriate action to ensure that everyone in the information centre will feel confident of their personal safety (especially if the centre is open longer and later than other facilities in the building or in the area). Make sure, too, that you comply with health and safety requirements, both in terms of the equipment that you use and in the design and maintenance of your facilities.

Acoustics

Don't be fooled into thinking that, because the old myth persists that libraries are quiet places, you don't need to pay any attention to the acoustics of your information centre. It's still important that your centre has suitable facilities for quiet research as well as areas where conversation can go on normally. Bindings and documents will absorb sound and hard surfaces reflect it. Can you arrange the layout so that the areas that need quieter conditions are not only convenient for fetching documents but are able to use the sound absorbing properties of the documents? At any rate, make sure that the everyday operation of the centre does not interfere with those users who need study facilities, or vice versa. Keep these issues in mind so far as possible when installing telephones and office machinery, although it is obvious that sometimes your choices will be limited by matters such as where the telephone lines have been installed.

Access

Not only is it a good idea to make sure that everyone has easy access to your centre, in many countries it's a legal obligation. In the UK, the Disability Discrimination Act sets out the rights of people with some kind of physical impairment to have access to public places, and this kind of legislation is found in many other countries.

Some of the factors you will need to address will also be things you need to take care of in order to meet other regulations. So if you leave ample room for any patrons who use a wheelchair, you will also meet the health and safety regulations designed to make sure everyone can leave safely if there is a fire. In other cases designing the centre for disabled access will make everyday life easier – for example, connecting different levels with ramps not only makes access easier, it helps you to move library materials around without having to lift heavy loads up steps.

Take advice on the design of your centre, either from within your community or by using an external source of help.

Maintaining your effort

Looking after all of these issues will take considerable effort on your part and that of your colleagues. Why let it go to waste after a few weeks of operation?

Make sure that the centre is maintained in a tidy, clean and safe condition. If it is locked at night, make sure that someone comes in during the day to clean it. Ensure that it is cleaned by people who understand how to care for the publications and other materials in it – no damp cloths or chemical cleaning sprays on precious papers! Ensure that repairs are carried out especially if you think that a piece of equipment or an area of the building is becoming unsafe. Find out how to keep the decorations fresh – many libraries go without being repainted for many years because the owners of the building think it is too big a job to move the stock or cover it up. If you are responsible for external access or surroundings, make sure that they are also tidy, inviting and safe. Have paths repaired, lawns cut and shrubs kept tidy so that they do not make the centre look tired or untidy, and do not risk injuring any of your users or potential users.

Sometimes you will feel that there are better things to do with your time, but it will ensure that your customers look forward to visiting your information centre and know that they will be coming to a pleasant and safe environment.

Summary

In this chapter we have looked at a variety of the questions you will need to address concerning the physical location and environment of your information centre. You will probably have to negotiate with other people to complete work on many of these questions but it is important that you do not overlook any of them. Making sure that everything is safe and tidy will reflect well on your centre and increase the use that is made of it, quite apart from ensuring that you comply with any legislation that affects you concerning access, security and the well-being of your customers and staff.

4

Staffing

● ●

In this chapter we look at the staffing requirements for
your information centre. We discuss:

- the kind of staff you will need
- the number of staff you will need
- managing staff budgets
- managing people – staff and management
- training staff
- building the perfect team
- reporting to management.

● ●

What kind of staff do you need?

To decide what kind of staff you need, you will need to identify the
requirements (or specification) for the services that you will be providing
to your internal and external customers. To do this, analyse the aims and
objectives of your organization or the description of your user community
(which you should be able to find in the organization's mission statement)
and translate it into a statement of purpose for your library or information
centre. This will enable the organization's aims and objectives to be ful-
filled or the community's needs to be met, and will also define what type
of staff (for instance the mix of levels of responsibility, and – as we shall
see below – the number of people) will be needed and what kind of
expertise they should have.

For example, you might decide that your users' needs could be met by the following activities and services:

- promoting awareness of the library and information centre
- providing an enquiry service
- providing guidance and advice
- supplying copies or loan copies of documents
- producing catalogues and bibliographies
- producing databases
- obtaining data from remote sources
- providing lists of references.

With your list completed, these tasks need to be analysed in more detail. Not only does this exercise enable you to define and achieve good standards in the various services, but it provides the basis for the job descriptions that you will adopt for each post. This will help you or your manager to decide what type of staff you should recruit, and what kind of expertise you will want them to have. It will be important to engage the right kind of person for each job, and to decide what level of training you want them to have achieved. Apart from the current requirements, for example, education to a particular level – maybe A-level for support staff, and graduate for professional staff – you should identify training needs, in the short term to carry out the main elements of the job and in the longer term to fulfil the wider role of the job.

Effective training should be:

- a systematic process, which is planned and controlled, but also includes learning from experience
- concerned with developing and improving the concepts, skills and attitudes of people considered as individuals and as groups
- aimed at improving performance in the person's present and possible future jobs
- through all of these, enhancing the effectiveness of the part of the organization where the individual or group works.

One way of grouping the staff for the efficient running of a library or information centre could be into the following three categories:

- **Office personnel** – people who do not necessarily have a professional qualification, but who have had some specialized training or experience in an information service. Educated to a high general standard, they usually perform tasks that support the activities of the information centre but do not require professional knowledge. They could for example process library materials, do routine compilation of bibliographic records, or manage security, accounting, circulation and personnel procedures.
- **Information officers or librarians** – staff members who have a professional qualification, usually a degree, in information science or librarianship. They will often have considerable autonomy in the planning and performance of their duties, which consist mainly of professional work such as carrying out detailed bibliographic searches, replying to enquiries, preparing abstracts and summaries, and, in larger units, supervising support staff.
- **Head or manager of the library or information centre** – a senior post responsible for the overall direction of the library or information centre, often with personal responsibility for planning, goal setting, preparation and monitoring of the budget, and for selection and review of some or all of the staff (depending on the size of the unit). The head of the unit should have graduate qualifications in either information studies or librarianship, which could be a postgraduate qualification after a subject-related first degree. The head of unit will also need experience in staff management, budgetary control and the selection, storage, retrieval and dissemination of information. Other desirable qualities include training skills, negotiating and diplomatic skills (that is, the ability to be both advocate and ambassador for the service).

How many staff do you need?

You clearly do not want to run a service where the staff sit around all day waiting for an enquiry to come in, but nor do you want one where the staff are so pressed for time that they are exhausted and do not have the time to handle all the work. So it's important to plan for the right number of staff – too few or too many and you will see people leave through overwork or boredom!

The ideal number may not be obvious at first, but the list of key tasks that you compiled earlier will provide the clues. Which tasks will be full time and which can be combined? Have you enough capacity to allow for people taking sick leave or annual leave? Will the service continue while the senior manager is out of the centre on leave or on business? (Of course it will, but who will take key decisions in his or her absence?)

In a small organization or business a single person may be expected to do every one of these tasks, in which case the decision is already taken and the issues are about providing access to the centre while the librarian is on leave. In centres with more than one member of staff, managerial responsibilities are likely to be added to the duties of one post. If instead two or more members of the information centre are managed individually by a person or persons outside the centre, the result is likely to be less good and it is worth arguing that the information centre staff should report through a single person with professional skills in order to ensure a consistent and professionally informed approach. If there is not enough work to move from one person to two, consider taking on a part time member of staff.

Managing staff budgets

While it may be generally true that work expands to fill the available capacity, business issues must be considered, for example, whether there is enough funding, and whether customer demands are justified. (So, are people asking appropriate questions or do they just like having a convenient and helpful source of information whether or not the business needs them to ask those particular questions? At the end of the day, people will have a higher opinion of the business skills in an information centre that turns down poorly justified requests for help.)

If there is real demand then the next issue is to define the level at which it is handled. Does research demand mean that the enquiries librarian or information specialist spends hours on the phone arranging the loan of items identified from databases? Is there a high level of walk-in users who need help to find information in reference books? Are demands made on the information centre's section heads to complete detailed monitoring, or to recruit staff for other sections of the organization? By taking the answers to these and other questions about the essential activities of the information centre and its staff, you will begin to recognize the level and number of staff needed.

Simple arithmetic can help you. Assume that people are effective for 90% of the time they are at work; the rest of the time they are taking comfort breaks or discussing television rather than the business. Then assess the time taken to carry out each task and use arithmetic to calculate how many people are needed. For example, if you handle 50 interlibrary loan requests a day and they take an average ten minutes to process, then you have a full time job for someone (one that you would probably share between two people if possible, to avoid total boredom for one person).

It gets more complicated where jobs can be open ended, such as dealing with enquiries. A simple counting system will not distinguish between the enquirer asking for the time of the next train to London, answered in 60 seconds, and the enquirer asking for a detailed clinical or engineering query to be answered through research. Here you will have to make an initial judgement and adjust the solution in the light of experience. Don't forget that you can hire temporary professional staff if you have a predictable peak of activity (maybe you are starting a new project that will run for six months) rather than taking on permanent staff who may then be under-employed.

Finally, will your chief manager enjoy the luxury of a focused job that consists entirely of management activities? If not, which tasks is he or she going to undertake as well? Do not assume that senior managers also have the skills to do the most complex searches, as they probably do not have up-to-date database specific training, and are better at 'big picture' activities. Finance and recruitment are likely to be better tasks for the centre manager to take on, and if responsibility for these is included in the job description then the deputy manager's job can be refined to attribute the right levels of responsibility to that post (for example, when the centre manager is on leave).

Finance will dictate the answers to some of these issues. If you have only £50,000 a year to spend on salaries and the associated costs, then you cannot afford five staff! The going rate may be dictated, for example, by agreements with trades unions or because there is an agreed scale, so you will need to assess your requirements against all these factors.

Using staff efficiently

A small college library was staffed by a single librarian who enjoyed the support of a part-time clerical assistant. This allowed the librarian to attend occasional meetings outside the library but complex enquiries could not be handled during his absence. The library had to close on occasions, for example for half of each day when the librarian was on annual leave or sick leave. The staff budget for this operation in 2004/5 was approximately £35,000 a year.

An assessment exercise found that there was justified demand for services to be available at all times, and that the sometimes unpredictable library closures were affecting the college's efficiency. An additional £10,000 a year was made available allowing a second part-time member of clerical staff to be taken on. This not only allowed the library to remain open all day during core term times but enabled the librarian to take a more prominent role in the community because he was confident that there were now the resources to cope with the additional demand his new networks would create. Although there was no more professional resource, the second clerical post took over some of the out of grade work done by the librarian, increasing job satisfaction for all concerned.

The UK employment tax regime includes complex requirements for the payment of national insurance contributions by the employer; these costs are reflected in similar employer taxes in other countries. It is beyond the scope of this book to explain them, but you should be aware that the true cost in financial terms alone of employing a member of staff is nearly 20% higher than the salary to be paid. Add to this the cost of paid holidays (for which you may need to buy in cover) and it becomes clear how important it is to set a realistic budget for staff costs. On top of this you might wish to consider contingency measures, such as how costs of any maternity leave, secondments, and other statutory or corporately sanctioned staff absences will be funded. Maybe it would be best to ask now rather than later if you need advice from your payroll or finance departments!

At the end of your deliberations you may end up with something like Table 4.1 as your staffing finance plan:

Table 4.1 Sample staffing finance plan

Staff member	Tenure	Cost in 2004/5
Centre manager	Permanent	£27,500
Assistant librarian	Permanent	£22,500
Assistant librarian	4 months for project	£7,500
Clerical assistant	Permanent, part time (0.5 FTE)	£7,500
	Staff cost for 2004/5	£65,000

This example shows that you might consider the alternative options of further clerical help in exchange for the cost of the short-term professional assistant, or that the project post is also vulnerable if in-year budget cuts are imposed.

Managing people – staff and management

While management training is absolutely not a waste of time, it cannot teach everything there is to know about being an effective manager, let alone a good one. So, some of the skills have to be learnt on the job. We have suggested that staff management experience is a quality you should look for in your senior team members, and they will learn more while working with you.

Many organizations have a management guide that sets out the qualities of good managers in their view, and many managers will find themselves being appraised against those qualities at the time of their annual reviews. There is still a view that information professionals are somehow excused from being managers because they have a specialism that takes the place of managerial skills. This is dangerous nonsense. Information centre staff need to be recognized as good managers of people and resources as this helps the reputation of the centre in the rest of the community, and helps it to be valued equally and taken seriously by the organization.

Detailed advice on good people management skills and techniques is outside the scope of this book but there is a wealth of good reading and courses available to help you. Consider those books and courses available from those working outside the information industry; managing people is a necessary skill in every industry sector, so a course that comes recommended by a colleague may be no less useful for being set in a context of chemical engineering if its lessons are universal or can be applied in information management. A fresh perspective can help to break through apparently impenetrable people management problems, so approach this issue with an open mind.

Our reading list includes a selection of titles that can help you to identify your requirements and to develop your people management skills.

Training information staff

Once you have recruited your staff, they will need training in the skills necessary for them to carry out their duties in the information centre. This applies to staff at all levels, regardless of their previous experience and professional knowledge. They will need to acquire a thorough knowledge of the function of the centre and the services that it offers. New staff may have specialist knowledge from previous experience of the routine work of an information centre, such as cataloguing, classification, enquiry services, but this needs to be supplemented by detailed information about the organization that they have just joined. Staff must have, or acquire, a detailed knowledge of the subject area. This training can be delivered through formal courses, through appropriate documentation, or a combination of both. This is particularly important for developing staff who have never worked on particular activities before, and you will find that it also helps with writing job descriptions.

So far as possible, identify what training will have to be run over the financial year and allocate funds to it. Where external courses have to be purchased, discover the costs and allocate these in advance, setting them against the available budget. So far as possible ensure that all staff who need training have access to it. This is important if your organization has submitted its training plans for accreditation, but is good practice anyway. Not all training is obtained by sending people on external courses for which you pay a fee, but much of the available professional development training is of this nature, meaning that you may have to negotiate quite hard for an adequate level of funding. It has become much easier in recent years to draw up a training plan since the major providers of training publish annual brochures listing their courses. (These used only to cover three to six months, making it hard to compile an annual plan.) Not only do these brochures identify the courses you will aim to send delegates to, but they identify the new areas that the training companies – based on their years of experience – believe will be the 'hot topics' for the coming year.

Continuing professional development

The concept of continuous professional development (CPD) requires individuals to ensure that their capabilities are enhanced throughout their working life in collaboration with their successive managers. Many organizations adopt CPD as a mandatory management activity both for the manager as participant and for the manager as a supporter of his or her staff. The new CILIP framework of qualifications supports CPD, as do initiatives from many professional bodies in the field of librarianship and information science. Take the time to investigate the current offerings in the field and to see how far the profession's views align with your organization's stance.

Building the perfect team
Why the team is so important

In many teams there will be someone who is 'intrapreneurial' – that is someone who looks for new ways of enhancing the services and promoting them to users and potential users within the organization. But even intrapreneurs must take some time away from the workplace. It is a good idea for everyone to recharge their batteries and take leave; and nobody is so indispensable that they must be at the workplace all day every day. Even if the intrapreneur is full of energy and never calls in sick, and even if they are running a one-person-show, there needs to be some kind of team that can provide backup. Holidays are not a luxury, and what about time to network within the organization or at the occasional conference or exhibition?

In larger organizations, the team is doubly important. The business of the library must continue while the team leader is away, and so developing a strong team is vital in order to provide a continuing service in line with the leader's vision.

Much is heard these days of ideas such as 'delayering' and the 'leaner, flatter' organization which became well known through Peters and Waterman (1982) in the 1980s. Organizations have been contracting – in both senses of the word. On the one hand, they call on external suppliers to make contracts to supply some services which were previously provided internally. On the other hand, organizations are shrinking. Public sector organizations have reduced in size. Private companies have had to trim in order to survive. Mergers are commonplace and so are the mergers of information functions that go along with them. New teams are formed, although some members of existing teams are lost, leading to new development needs to address the new organization's goals and team dynamics. Sometimes there are real shocks as small teams and large ones come together and find they have very different ways of working.

There are certainly advantages to team working, apart from the simple issues of continuity of presence and cover. Complex work plans are carried out better by teams; they can cover a wider range of roles than the individual, they provide quality assurance for each other, and they can ensure that goals are reached even when other important issues intervene. Team members feed off each other's ideas and develop typically more complex and successful solutions to problems than do individuals working alone. And teams can send stronger signals of commitment and involvement in the solution of organizational problems than individuals can do.

Skills and knowledge

We said earlier that some information professionals believe that their professional skills excuse them from being managers or team players, but we talk in this book about skills that belong as much in the boardroom or the council chamber as in the library or information centre. So in what follows it would be as well to assume a high level of professional skill as an essential requirement. After all, no matter how astute the management skills and however artful the political skills of the manager, unless he or she can deliver the goods when results are needed against deadlines, there will not be a second chance to use them.

We have previously proposed the concept of the intrapreneurial librarian. One such person can make a difference, while a team of like-minded and similarly skilled people can be formidable. In a small organization where the library gets to select its own staff, it should be possible to form a team that will follow a like-minded entrepreneurial path. This is, sadly, not always the case in larger organizations and the public sector in particular; but at least it is becoming more widely known that the library is not a good dumping spot for inefficient clerical staff who like reading.

Gifford Pinchot (n.d.) offers ten commandments for the intrapreneur, which give us a starting point in considering the skills that team members require. We are looking as much for a state of mind as for definable skills, and for an attitude to the task in hand as much as for detailed technical knowledge. Perhaps fortunately for the intrapreneurial librarian, the position of the library within many organizations saves the need to go out on a limb from the outset. Despite Pinchot's exhortation to come to work each day prepared to be fired, most librarians are probably safe from this fate given the kind of activity they tend to undertake and the organization's view of the risk it poses. On the other hand, the organizational structure that tends to surround libraries can prevent some of the more freewheeling approaches, such as forming teams of volunteers to work on risky projects.

These 'high-risk' elements aside, Pinchot's commandments suggest some useful characteristics for team members, and some new ways of working. Team members should be willing to turn their hand to any task needed to bring success to a library project. It is no good trying to run a dynamic, go-getting service with people whose go-getting dynamism stops dead when their support staff are on leave, or see some work as beneath or beyond them. Work with the best – and the best people are flexible people.

We also talked earlier about job descriptions. These are useful for saying what people should do, but they are less use for defining what they should not do. Short of doing things that provoke a strike, the members of a small library or information centre should be prepared to turn their hands to the whole range of tasks. If everyone else is busy, and the job has a deadline, then only one person can do the job; it's that simple. Pinchot notes the principle widely attributed to the Jesuits, that it is easier to ask for forgiveness than for permission, although it would be as well not to make a habit of this.

Hard work is called for. One of the problems of developing innovative services is that the main service needs to be kept going while the development takes place so you will be looking for flexibility and versatility in team members as a minimum. They will need to be good with people. They will need to convince others – often the movers and shakers – of the value of information, and to do so in a persuasive rather than a confrontational way. The movers and shakers of the organization, of the community, of whatever client group the library serves, those people can provide the library with enormous support if they are well served and publicly acknowledge the value of the library service.

Managing the team

Hierarchical organizations may have trouble managing intrapreneurial teams. These tend to work in a lateral kind of way, which upsets organizations that like to see instructions and responses travelling up and down a chain of command; intrapreneurs prefer to work in a way that cuts across hierarchies and structures in order to pull together teams of the people best suited to the task in hand. Organizations have had to change, however. Many sections of a large organization now have an interest in major projects, and success of a project often depends on the skills and knowledge of a number of people. The information technology function is often seen as critical; so too is the information management function, which complements it and which the librarian has first claim to manage. And how surprising if that librarian turns out to have been the first to adopt the new ways of working!

Organizations will generally demand that someone be recognized as in charge and responsible for the library or information unit. Skilful analysis of the role of the unit will allow delegation to those best able to lead work on particular issues and functions, so that they can lead task forces on those topics. A number of skills may need to be developed in these team leaders: handling inter-personal relationships, leadership and communication skills are examples. Team members need to be able to fulfil a number of roles in the teams, sometimes as leaders, sometimes in other roles. If formal project management techniques are used, team members will need to fill the stipulated roles in those techniques. In other cases, they may need to speak for the library alongside technical or user representatives. They need to have the confidence not only of the library management but the organizational management in doing so, and it is important that necessary training should be provided either through courses or through coaching by taking part, under guidance and supervision, in existing projects.

Team playing beyond the information and library service

Knowledge management is widely recognized as a team enterprise. In addition to the information service teams described above, there is value in forming peer knowledge networking teams across an organization or community – that is, teams that are formed at high level to combine skills and specialist knowledge of different areas, and which may operate on a basis closely resembling continuous brainstorming.

Other specialists, managers and professionals will balance the information and library service manager's less developed areas of knowledge, and his or her specialisms will in turn balance other managers' shallower knowledge in the field of information management.

All members of an information and library service should be given the opportunity to take part in such community-wide committees and boards. Not only is it good development experience, but their differing interpretations of the same events in the wider world will provide further grist for the management team to direct the service.

Users demand co-ordinated services, and are uninterested in which part is supplied by a library professional and which by an IT specialist. Many modern library services rely on IT to the point where it is unclear which is the information content and which is the communication technology. Much of what modern librarians do could not be done without information technology.

Yet many of the enquiries put to library professionals make no use of their information management skills but are concerned rather with issues such as making printers work or dealing with slow communication from a remote database or the internet. It makes good sense in many libraries to manage library IT and library user services within a single team. Yet it is a considerable management problem. On the one hand, the library service must be run competently and professionally, so IT staff without formal library training must be given basic knowledge to allow them to handle simple library enquiries correctly and fully. The other requirement is that library staff have sufficient IT knowledge to deal with some simple, and maybe some more complex, problems, while not feeling that their library professional qualifications are being squandered. Since the staff numbers involved are often quite small, for example when academic libraries cover late evening working with mixed profession teams of this kind, solutions are essential. They are based on a more general consideration of the principles underlying successful team management that could easily apply to management generally.

Monthly reports to management

Once everything is in place and running, the centre manager will find it useful to compile a monthly report both for the benefit of senior management or the supplier of funding, and for the centre staff themselves to interpret. This report should give a continuous narrative on the developments of the centre, and the following measures (below) could be used to highlight the results of the activities. The report can also be used to emphasize achievements and also any problems that may be emerging.

There is constant debate about what are useful measures of activity. While agreement is rare, it is generally held that ratios are more use than simple counting of things that move. Thus, rather than stating the number of loans, it may be interesting to state the number of people who were provided with loans in the last month and to say what proportion of the total user base they represent and how many items each they borrowed on average. So where the report could have said simply that '216 items were borrowed in January', more useful performance information would have been given by saying for example 'in January requests were received from 32 members of staff out of a total of 128 in the company (25%) and they were lent 216 items, an average of 6.75 items per person (up from 6.3 in December) with the highest number being 12 items to support one person on a training course'. Detail such as this is often quickly available from automated housekeeping systems, and can be supplemented with anecdote to provide an interesting and arresting report that shows the value of the service. You will no doubt choose your measures to show the information centre in the best light, and will investigate the weaker areas of performance so that when challenged you will know why they are weak and what you are doing about it!

We suggest some measures that can be collected are:

- use of the library
  — number of requests for information – how long it took to answer the enquiries (perhaps categorized by time bands)
  — number of loans
  — number of photocopies
  — number of new acquisitions (which by purchase, exchange, etc.)
  — number of visitors, telephone calls, e-mails
  — comparisons with similar periods
- any training courses or special events attended or organized by the information centre staff
- financial situation – summary of expenditure and position against budget profile
- staffing situation including current and anticipated vacancies
- publications produced, e.g. centre newsletter, leaflets, etc.

Find out the underlying figures such as the number of potential users in the total population so that you can start to prepare useful comparisons.

Your reports could form the basis of meetings with senior managers or a library committee.

Summary

In this chapter we have examined some of the issues concerning team working in the information and library service. We have found that two kinds of team are required :

- a team of matched individuals working within the information and library service, who between them can provide the skills and experience to match the customers' needs, and go on to provide innovative, entrepreneurial service
- a team outside the information and library service in which the head (or other members) of the service take part, and which drives forward concepts such as knowledge management. This provides the information and library service with channels outward for its views and contributions, and channels inward for information about events affecting the organization it serves and the people who are its customers.

5

Information networks

● ●

In this chapter we examine:

- the concept of networks
- local and regional information sources
- national and international information resources
- centres of excellence – subject information resources
- print-based information sources
- electronic information sources.

● ●

In this chapter we look at information networks that will support your service, making it easier for you to provide services to your users at the most economical costs. Some are formal, some less so. If you make use of these resources you will be able to devote your own funding to obtaining the key materials that your information service must provide, and use networks and external sources to provide more marginal materials. Because we are writing about a wide range of library and information services, we cannot mention every subject resource but you will probably find links to these resources from some of those that we mention below. And although this book is written primarily from a British viewpoint, we aim to provide useful links for any reader who is searching for suitable help.

All forms of network, if used and managed effectively, can provide the route to tomorrow's successful information service. The information professional must keep pace with the converging technologies of print, computer, film, video, sound and telecommunications. But the personal and personnel networks are equally, if not more, important and they are sometimes forgotten in the technological mêleé.

Given that the world today is really one big global electronic information village, where can the information professional find ways of sustaining and developing to ensure success not only for themselves, but for others, for instance the organization and – the most important factor – the customer? The answer must surely be in networking – of every variety!

What is a network?

The term 'network' is defined variously as:

- an interconnected group or system
- a system of intersecting lines, roads or veins
- another name for 'net', which is defined also as an open work fabric or string wire mesh, or a device made of net
- a means to protect or enclose things or to trap animals.

It is perhaps the first two definitions above that have the most meaning in information and library work. Without networks and networking many services that we offer today would not survive. Networking in library and information services (LIS) is an essential feature if there is commitment to providing a good quality information service. Networking enhances the basic services by providing quicker routes to the acquisition of a piece of information for a customer. Information staff will recognize this way of getting information without necessarily realizing that it is part of the networking concept.

The practice starts early in the professional information worker's career once they leave their university of information studies. The young professionals will keep in touch with each other and as necessity arises will telephone, fax or e-mail each other with and for information. This is most likely to occur if the young professional is working alone, where there will be a need to keep in touch, not only for informational needs but to avoid professional isolation. So networking can be used for personal, professional and technical needs.

Some 'must have' personal skills to be able to network successfully

There are a number of wide ranging personal skills that you need to develop to be able to network successfully. You will need communications skills, including telephone skills, meeting skills, presentational skills, good listening skills, writing skills, time management skills, team member or solo player skills, leadership skills, marketing knowledge, a flair for publicity, to be in the right place at the right time and to be able to deliver the right kind of information at the right time (if not before it is needed).

How does a network originate?

There is no simple answer to this question. Sometimes networks form naturally, other times they will be formally set up.

There can be any number of people or organizations involved in a network. Likewise, any level of people may participate. The reasons for a network are endless. Sometimes they centre on a single issue, other times a political issue. Often it will be necessary to ensure that there is easy access to individuals, organizations or information.

Many kinds of network exist and these can be formal or informal, and literally occur anywhere, as illustrated below.

Local and regional information sources
Inside organizations

Networking inside the organization is essential, particularly if the information service is to be the centre of the organization (and in particular if the information service is to develop). Typical networking opportunities arise through membership of various committees and this cuts across divisions or branches in an organization. An example would be a computer strategy committee that looks at the future computer requirements, which involves information provision. There are many similar opportunities in an organization to establish good personal contacts with mutual benefits to both parties.

The information service in an organization will frequently find that, in addition to its normal function, it also has an internal information exchange role and thus becomes the hub of a network. The benefits to the information service are enormous, giving them advantages that perhaps no other branch or division may have within the organization.

Local information networks

These networks exist in a variety of forms: formal or informal, meeting face to face, or by e-mail, telephone, fax or letter.

If you cannot provide particular resources for the users of your service, then it is useful both for them and for you if you have arrangements with another nearby service that will enable you to obtain the required information. This could be either by borrowing it or by linking your users into the location where it is held.

There are many local groups that allow library and information professionals to make contact with others nearby. They vary in their formality and the way that they are organized. CILIP: the Chartered Institute of Library and Information Professionals, has recently reorganized the structure of its branch network and may make further changes. The Institute of Information Scientists had a strong regional structure and this has been carried into the new body, strengthening CILIP's own regional organization. Regular meetings take place in locations across the UK where library and information professionals can hear presentations on topics of interest and, most importantly, take the opportunity to network and socialize with others and thus build personal networks of colleagues in other organizations.

Special interest groups

Many information professionals belong to CILIP; however, they may also need to set up a network of their interests in a particular subject group, and the British and Irish Association of Law Librarians (BIALL) is an example of this. Equally there is a possibility that the format of the information work may draw individuals to want or need to set up a specialized network. A good example of this is the various online groups which were set up in the late 1970s. These online groups recognized that there was a need for a central group focusing naturally on particular topical areas, so the UK Online Users Group 'UKOLUG' was formed; this is now UKeiG – the UK e-information Group.

Subject groups offer you the opportunity to build a network of professionals in other organizations with similar interests to your own. You may be concerned, if you work in a commercial environment, that you could find yourself in a difficult situation as regards commercial confidentiality. Just as you would not divulge your company's trade secrets to competitors, so you would not expect them to tell you theirs; but specialist information groups thrive on members who abide by the library and information professional code of ethics in their dealings. Information services of competing companies are often able to provide a link to mutual benefit while respecting each other's commercial sensitivities.

There are local groups with subject specialisms, and local groups that bring together staff from particular kinds of libraries and information centres. The growth of easy access to web-authoring tools and cheap hosting means that the world wide web is the obvious and easy first place to research your local groups. You can also find some local meetings listed in the professional press, such as *Library and Information Gazette* (which is available to members of CILIP).

A number of library schools around the world include lists on their web pages, while CILIP not only lists its special interest groups and regional branches but has a separate list of what are called Organisations in Liaison, or OiLs. These OiLs include specialist library groups that are not special interest groups but independent groups which have a special relationship with CILIP. These offer the opportunity to meet others with similar personal interests or characteristics.

Co-operatives

Over the years much has been written on co-operatives, why they exist and their long-term benefits. One of the earliest examples is the UK's SINTO (Sheffield Interchange Organization), which started in 1932 and is still going strong because the members who are representatives of the organizations involved are still committed to the early reasons for the establishment of the group (SINTO, n.d.).

Co-operatives have stood the test of time. Not only are usual benefits gained, such as interlending items, acquiring photocopies, and getting information quickly and cost effectively, but also other benefits such as promoting each other's services, mutual training courses and visits to each other's organization to gain knowledge of stock and services.

It is often advantageous within these formal groups to set up informal subgroups to move particular tasks along.

Library and information plans (LIPs): the new(er) networks

Library and information plans are an old idea given modern packaging. This time round there is a commercial look to the idea; they are intended to add value to services, and cost per unit.

A library and information plan is a statement to its users of what the library/information service is intending to achieve in forthcoming years. It will span two to three years ahead, and will need constantly revising. It will include: what the organization aims to achieve; the role of the library/information service within the wider goals of the organization; the needs of users; development of services, including those that are technology-based; projected costs of equipment, materials, acquisitions, building and refurbishment; outlay on communications; budgets for training of staff and users; and publicity and promotion.

The library and information plan will be closely integrated with the long-term business plan of the parent organization or community, but will make a strong statement about the role of the library and information service within that body.

Community information networks

Community information networks exist for members to share experiences and knowledge with each other. Many such networks have emerged over the past few years, from Freenets in the USA and Canada, to a host of others around the world; they are popular in the UK. Community Information Network conferences and seminars held in Sheffield from 1995 onwards are described in *Building Community Information Networks* (Pantry, 1999).

Training networks

Good training and education underpin good services. It is essential that all information staff, continually update their skills. It is also recognized that users need training and education in information retrieval. Sessions on offer could range for example, from learning about multimedia or legal information to training in the use of the internet for information for businesses.

The benefits gained from this network membership are enormous. It keeps information managers up to date with local developments, allows them to act as a member of a pressure group if appropriate, and enables them to share training costs and to attend local seminars instead of going on expensive journeys.

Online networks

Arguably one of the most exciting events in the information world in the last two decades has been the emergence of computers and associated technologies which have enabled many tasks to be streamlined and, at the same time, given opportunities to improve services and, most importantly, offer new services to users.

In the early 1970s when online services were in their infancy, not too many library and information services were active in this area. Consequently it was a natural step to take to set up online user groups around the UK. These groups largely comprised kindred spirits struggling against all odds to understand this innovative way of retrieving information. The members of these online groups set up (and still do set up) meetings to enable the online database hosts, database producers, equipment suppliers and software specialists to demonstrate their wares. They also assisted in training and enlightening information specialists about the wonder of 'the new world' of having quick and easy access to vast and ever-increasing amounts of information.

As members of these networks began to realize that not everything was so wonderful, they became pressure groups exhorting telecommunication organizations, database hosts, and so on, to improve their services. Inevitably a national UK online group was formed to give extra emphasis to the requirements of information service providers.

Virtual worlds – electronic networks

Virtual information resources centres can be created by individuals for individuals. This takes the information manager out of the walls and possibly the constraints of the existing information centre or library and enables him or her to be able to offer to customers a tailor-made service. For example, the chief executive of an organization may wish to receive on his computer a selection of the world's press on a particular subject. Establishing a profile on the world's news services such as Reuters, Press

Association, CNN and so on will enable the steady flow of selected information to be delivered in a format that can be re-used if necessary. The information service may wish to 'top and tail' the daily delivery with their own logo and headings – just to ensure that the chief executive remembers where the information is coming from.

Delivering information this way ensures that the busy customer receives the information at the pace required, which can be pulled up on the screen whenever it is wanted. Timescales are important when networking so the information professional will need to decide each time what is really urgent and what can be delivered at a more leisurely pace. Remember that if you constantly pressure others in networks, you may eventually lose some friends.

CD-ROM networks

The term 'network' takes a new meaning where CD-ROMs are concerned. It is now possible to network CD-ROMs – have CD-ROMs that were previously only available for use on a single personal computer to be networked (in the computer sense) across an information service or organization. This enables many people to have access to single CD-ROMs.

Action group networks

The Standing Committee on Official Publications (SCOOP) is a good example of an action group. It aims to:

- improve the access to, and availability of, UK official publications
- identify problems in the provision of access to UK official publications, in particular their bibliographic control and distribution
- make proposals for possible solutions to problems in the provision of access to UK official publications
- provide a mechanism for the exchange of views on matters of common interest to the library and information community concerning UK official publications
- provide a forum with The Stationery Office (TSO) for the constructive discussion of services provided by TSO for the library and information community

- take the necessary steps to keep the library and information profession informed of their deliberations.

Discussions with HMSO since the inception of the SCOOP in 1971 have resulted in many changes and considerably enhanced services for librarians. SCOOP was very much involved in the 1996 privatization of HMSO (now TSO). In 2005, HMSO was absorbed into the Office of Public Sector Information (OPSI) within the Cabinet Office. SCOOP maintains regular contact with both TSO and OPSI, and is consulted about changes and developments and the views of the library and information community in the UK and the wider world. SCOOP is a standing committee of the Information Services Group (ISG) of CILIP.

National and international information resources

Your service will never have either the money to buy or the room to store every publication that your users might want. The answer is to make use of one or more of the information resources available at national or international level. You will need to budget for the cost of using these services, either on each occasion that you make use of them, or by purchasing subscriptions.

National documentation centres

In the UK, the British Library has long been the supplier of documents from its extensive stock through the Document Supply Centre located at Boston Spa, West Yorkshire. It has a range of services to suit all clients, whether or not they have an account. Paper and electronic documents are available, and items can be identified and ordered online.

Similar services can be identified in other countries, for example CISTI in Canada, INIST in France or the National Library of Australia Document Supply Service. However, the development of electronic services has made it less important to deal with the centre that is geographically nearest to your location, so that you could opt instead to go to a national centre for the country of publication of an item you are interested in, and then order it using a credit card to pay for reproduction, copyright clearance and delivery.

The range of materials available from these national centres has expanded considerably from the classic service, which offered only copies of periodical articles and books on loan. The Australian National Library's Copies Direct service (Australian National Library, n.d.) offers copies of journal articles, chapters of books, photographs, pictures, maps, manuscripts, music and sound recordings. The copies are posted to the Library's website and a password is sent to the user who can then unlock and view the content. Alternatively the item can be e-mailed, or reproduced in a conventional medium and posted to the recipient.

The British Library's Secure Electronic Delivery (SED; British Library, n.d.) service works similarly, with a website where encrypted Portable Document Format (PDF) copies of documents are posted for the user to access and unlock using the key provided. PDFs are marketed by Adobe (**www.adobe.com**).

International information resources

International networks

Examples of international networks abound, for example, the International Labour Organisation Occupational Safety and Health (OSH) Centre has its headquarters in Geneva, and is linked to over 137 countries around the world each with an established national or collaborating centre. These centres are based in industrial countries, emerging European democracies and developing countries. The goal of all centres is to be the focal point in their own country and to act as a link in the network to enable occupational health and safety information to be easily sourced, disseminated and exchanged internationally.

The concept of 'twinning' was introduced a few years ago by the UK national centre to enable newly established centres achieve their goals more quickly by learning from the more experienced 'twin'. This kind of networking promotes training, helps with the acquisition of information and also enables ideas to be exchanged quickly.

E-mail networks

Having access to electronic mail internationally also assists information professionals to be able easily and quickly to get information from across the world. This also benefits the end users. By setting up reciprocal agreements, an information centre can automatically receive new information without costs. This type of exchange agreement saves staff time in not having to pursue newly published information.

European Union networks

In recent years there has been the need to have a European Union (EU) network in a variety of information subjects, such as networks of OSH, legal, national and regional. A good example in the European Agency for Safety and Health at Work, which has a focal information point in each member state. This enables exchange and contact for information within a particular country for up-to-date information.

The 'invisible college'

One of the most intriguing types of networks is the 'invisible college'. It exists in all professions and cuts across all levels and organizations. No one really knows how it starts; it does not meet on any specific occasion yet it is very effective. Often erroneously confused with the 'old boy' network, it is a rather superior type of peer group whose members do not really know each other! Nevertheless it is a very efficient means of putting people in touch with other people.

Centres of excellence – subject information resources

Specialist subject collections offer the answer to some information needs in a way that the smaller information centre cannot hope to emulate. There is no real purpose in trying to duplicate a collection to which access can readily be gained by subscription or free access, since using that collection for any requirements other than a core set of documents (those that your users will need regularly and frequently) does not make economic sense. Only if it is essential for you to create a second collection similar or even identical to a national resource should you begin to build it. Even then you may care to reflect on the implications of doing so, as you might find people asking for access to your collection, or others asking why you have taken this line – especially if you are publicly funded. There are specialist collections, public and private, in a wide range of subject fields.

Collections in centres of excellence in the UK

Local government

Local government public libraries often turn out to have valuable resources where they have inherited the collections of societies and trade associations within their boundaries. The City of London Libraries have a number of such collections, as might be expected. But there are some surprises. The City Libraries house not only the Gardeners' Company collection of historic works on gardening and a number of other collections related to trades and crafts. The Libraries also shelter the International Food and Wine Society Library, the Institute of Masters of Wine Library and the personal collections of the food writers André Simon, Jane Grigson and Jeremy Round.

Academic and charitable libraries

The Women's Library, London (**www.thewomenslibrary.ac.uk**) is a well-known women's history collection; it is part of London Metropolitan University but is also a registered charity that has friends and patrons schemes to help support it.

A number of collections are indexed on the websites of umbrella organizations, such as What's in London Libraries (WiLL; **www. londonlibraries. org.uk**), bringing together details of special collections in public and other libraries that are accessible through the Libraries and Learners in London scheme; see **www.londonlibraries.org/servlets/ llil/specialist** for list of specialist libraries in the scheme) or the Association of Independent Libraries (AIL, n.d.). An index to a number of relevant websites (from across the world) is included in the Open Directory project (Open Directory, n.d.).

Directories of libraries and information resources will provide you with further information. *The New Walford* (Lester, 2005, 2006, 2007), published by Facet between 2005 and 2007, will provide up-to-date information in a wide range of subject areas.

Print-based information sources

We looked earlier at national libraries and document delivery services, but there are other print-based information sources that you can draw on. There are still some subscription libraries that can help you by providing access to their resources to supplement your own. The suitability of these resources will depend on your users' requirements, of course, but a subscription to a suitable library could either give you access to a wider range – perhaps historical, perhaps current publications outside your current core subject area – or allow you to deal with peak demand by borrowing additional copies of popular titles rather than having to buy multiple copies that will later go to waste.

The London Library

The London Library is an independent library that has operated since 1841, and has over a million volumes at its London premises in St James's Square. Its collection is founded in the humanities and arts, especially history, biography, literature, art, religion and philosophy. It does not cover business, law or technology although it does cover their histories. Institutions, associations, organizations and commercial bodies are able to take out 'representational membership', which allows them to borrow up to ten books at a time (15 items if the organization is located more than 20 miles from the Library) and additional subscription options allow for greater numbers of books to be borrowed at once. Charities benefit from a reduced subscription and public libraries also enjoy beneficial terms. For many smaller organizations membership of this or another library may make sound economic sense if it allows readers to have wider access to publications of interest. Although only one 'new' book (one published in the last four months) may be held at a time, this could still be enough to make it worth the £460 annual subscription (2005 price). The Library also holds a number of periodicals, which could also be of interest to potential subscribers.

Electronic information sources

The growth of the world wide web has supported the growth of resources for the library and information community. This has not just been in terms of enabling information delivery through the websites of document aggregators who provide access to full text journals and other publications.

The web allows the publication of links and commentaries guiding users to the required information. Resource discovery can be a time-consuming business but by using a suitable portal the staff of a new information service can rapidly locate suitable information to meet patrons' needs.

The UK's Resource Discovery Network (RDN; **www.rdn.ac.uk**) is an excellent example of this type of website (see Figure 5.1). It catalogues and links to around 60,000 other sites that are considered worthwhile resources in their subject fields. It also links to other portal sites for a range of subjects in the humanities and sciences. A search engine allows further research among the many links provided, including several hundred to other library networks.

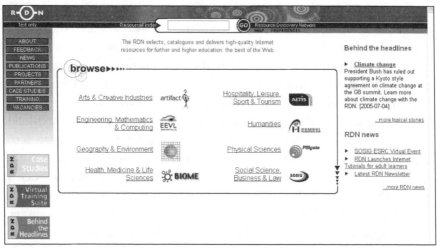

Figure 5.1   A page on the Resource Discovery Network website

General search engines are another means of locating information resources, and should not be dismissed just because your users are likely to have tried them too. The power of the leading search engines such as Google makes them useful sources for information professionals; the professional skill is to use them by careful selection of search terms, and by adapting the search strategy in the light of the results returned. However, the library and information professional knows how to use a range of search tools and information resources to retrieve relevant material in electronic form. These include:

- the full range of world-class search engines (such as Google, AltaVista and Yahoo!)

- metasearch engines (such as Ixquick or AskJeeves), which run your query against several other search engines and return consolidated results – some, like AskJeeves, can cope with natural language queries as well as strings of search terms
- 'deep web' resources – sites that are not indexed by search engines and therefore need to be searched separately, typically dynamic websites that are built by content management systems
- weblogs, a growingly important resource consisting of personal commentaries on events posted by individuals to the world wide web and sometimes revealing insights into competitors or into public organizations.

Search engines fall into two major types: those that will search the web for a given word or phrase, and those that categorize websites using a hierarchical directory structure. Google is the best known of the true search engines, while these days a search using a directory structure is best carried out on the site of the Open Directory Project (**www.dmoz.org**). Many search engines nowadays share a common database of websites and links, since it is very costly to maintain the information. There are many regional and specialist engines; if you need more than the best of the international engines can provide, look at the links available from commentators such as Search Engine Watch (**http://searchenginewatch.com/links/**).

Make sure that your users know that your information centre offers them improved access to all these electronic resources, as well as to any electronic journals that you purchase. You may well be able to locate a number of suitable free resources, as some newsletters and journals can be obtained without payment. Use your page on the local intranet to allow your users to find the links in one easy place – but be careful about publishing the links on the internet until you have obtained permission from the publisher to include their details.

Summary

This chapter has looked briefly at a number of ways for you to tap into information networks to support your information service. We have seen that these networks include national and international resources, and that people are as much a resource as information centres are. We have also discussed some electronic resources, and looked at the specialist libraries that can support you for a modest subscription.

In the reading lists section we include details of the major associations for library and information professionals that are likely to be of interest to readers in Europe, North America, Australia and New Zealand; you can find links on our associated website to a number of smaller associations and specialist library groups in the UK. The website also includes links to the main search engines.

No doubt the reader will be convinced that networking really does provide benefits, some tangible, others hard to quantify. As a long time network enthusiast, there is the necessity to keep pace with the converging technologies. All skills must be continually updated, to ensure that your own network can be reached by whatever means and wherever the individual contact is located. *So . . . networking for success is possible for everyone!*

6

Services to be provided by the library and information service

● ●

This chapter looks at the services to be provided by your library and information service. Libraries provide a wide range of services to their users and you will wish to provide many if not all of them. This chapter includes information about:

- acquisitions (printed and electronic materials)
- organizing information
- indexes and indexing
- abstracts and abstracting
- how to build up a database
- enquiry services
- loan services
- periodicals
- reference collections
- disseminating information
- translation and interpreting services
- standards and response times
- other services tailored to particular user groups.

● ●

Acquisitions

The term 'acquisitions' is used to cover the procurement of bibliographic materials by purchase, exchange or gift. It includes pre-order searching (to identify the right item or items), ordering and receiving materials, processing invoices for payment, and keeping necessary records. Purchases can be made direct from publishers or producers although many centres prefer to use intermediaries, such as subscription agents or book dealers, who do most of the work of locating the items they need. Acquiring materials can be done individually, piece by piece, or based on a long-term acquisitions plan, but this will depend on the budget allocated to the information centre or library. As a result of the information audit the information manager will know the type of acquisition that the customers need, and after research will also know the costs of supplying these needs.

Using a subscription agent

If you have a list of more than a few journals that you wish to purchase, contact one or more subscription agents. They will be able to cost the list of journals that you wish to purchase. The advantage of using an agent is that they are able to take on much of the detailed work in ordering and also chase overdue deliveries, thus relieving you these chores which can be very time-consuming. You can expect to receive some small discount off the price of journals, but are also likely to have to pay service charges as the agent works on smaller margins than in the bookselling trade.

One useful service offered by agents is generally known as 'consolidation'; this is where the agent marks in each issue of the journal and attaches any circulation lists (the names and locations of the people who see the journal before it is sent to be shelved) before sending you a parcel containing a day's or a week's issues. The advantage of this for a small information centre is that it saves the work of checking in and of chasing missing issues, but the down side is that there are extra charges and you may have to wait slightly longer for journals to arrive.

Using a local book supplier

Your local book suppliers may be willing to offer you discounts if you are likely to be spending a certain amount of the budget each year with them on acquisitions. Be clear how much you can afford to put with them, and consider that this will be a contractual deal – you are morally and probably legally bound to keep your side of the deal. It may be more difficult for them to offer you big discounts on academic or non-fiction titles than on best selling fiction. There remain a number of library booksellers, including specialists dealing in (for example) legal or foreign titles – but numbers have dwindled recently as takeovers and mergers have brought previously separate booksellers together. If you are allowed to use internet booksellers, there are good deals to be had on a range of publications, although again expect better offers on best selling titles.

Buying newspapers

Buying newspapers is a specialist business in itself: if you need a few national daily papers, then your local newsagent is as good a bet as any, and may give you a discount for a large and regular order. If you need large supplies each day, and especially if you want them pre-addressed to individual members of your organization, then you would do better to get in touch with one of the specialist news suppliers. They have standard discounts and you should ask whether your order would qualify for any reduction.

Exchanges

There are two kinds of material exchanges: direct and duplicate. Direct exchanges occur when an information centre sends specified materials to another centre in exchange for materials of similar value. Duplicate exchanges occur when a centre makes its duplicate, unwanted materials available to other centres in exchange for their duplicates. Direct exchange may be the only way to acquire certain materials, particularly from foreign countries.

To enable the exchanges to take place you will need to identify appropriate government departments, organizations, institutions, universities, and so on. Contact them to describe your community's interests and to say what materials you produce that might be suitable for exchange. Gift materials can sometimes arrive in your information centre without your sending a request or expressing any interest. Usually they arrive singly or as a mixed batch, but they could also consist of large quantities of materials collected by someone and then donated as a collection. Bear in mind that a subject specialist within your organization might propose an exchange, or that you might receive items through multi- or bi-lateral technical co-operation between similar organizations. It may be that setting up your information centre is the trigger for someone to donate the collection of publications that they have been receiving from an overseas partner for many years, when that person didn't know what to do with them!

Organizing information

Books, reports, standards, legal documents, journals, videos, DVDs and electronically held documents (the collection) must be organized for use by customers who have direct access to the collection and to facilitate the work of information officers or librarians. An important part of collection organization is the preparation of bibliographic records that conveniently describe and represent the collection items themselves. The records may then be organized and made available for use; the material must be labelled so that it can be stored consistently. Therefore, organization consists of indexing the information, preparing bibliographic abstracts, arranging them in a catalogue or database, and placing the items on shelves or other suitable storage locations, in a predetermined, useful order. These processes are commonly grouped together under the term 'cataloguing and classification', but there are many variations of these traditional activities. Normally every item which is purchased by the centre should be recorded, whether held in the centre or acquired for an individual for long-term loan. Recorded means making a catalogue or database entry relating to the item, and classifying it. The basic functions of the centre's catalogues or databases are to:

• list the contents of the collection
• provide information for guidance to the user in the selection of items most likely to suit his or her needs
• inform the user of the location of those items
• assist the information centre staff to find items to satisfy users' needs.

Without a good catalogue or database of the centre's information stock, a proportion of the information will effectively be lost, because no one will be able to find it. Cataloguing or indexing involves listing:

• the title
• the author(s), both personal and corporate

- the edition
- the publisher's name and the place where the item was published
- the date of publication
- the name of the series (if there is one)
- the ISBN (International Standard Book Number) or ISSN (International Standard Serial Number (for books and serials, respectively)
- notes including details of the format if appropriate
- keywords and abstract
- the type of document (report, book, standard, and so on)
- the location or filing instructions, number of copies
- the date added to database.

The Anglo-American Cataloguing Rules

There is a standard format (*Anglo-American Cataloguing Rules*, 2nd edition, or '*AACR2*', which is widely adopted in English language and other collections). *AACR2* sets out the order of the elements in the entry, and either mandates or guides the cataloguer in terms of how information is expressed. This can be fairly uncomplicated, such as as the instruction to put the author's surname or family name before the given or first name and separate them with a comma, or more complex depending on the element of description. *AACR2* is adopted in the UK, Canada, the USA and Australia, and fully or partly by 56 other countries, according to the British Library, whose website (**www.bl.uk/services/bibliographic/ catstandards.html**) gives more details of the standards adopted there. There are other cataloguing codes, but you will probably find that any specialist cataloguers you approach have trained using *AACR2*, and by adopting it you will make it easier to ensure that your catalogue is consistent and helpful to your users.

Using a database

It is useful for a catalogue to be created in computerized format – as a database – so searches may be carried out as efficiently as possible. It helps users if documents are classified or otherwise organized in some way, which allows searches by author or by the subject area. There are a number of widely used schemes such as the Universal Decimal Classification (UDC, British Standard 1000), which is used in specialist libraries, or the

Dewey Decimal Classification System, used by most public libraries and suitable for many small collections. Classification schemes provide code numbers that are assigned to each document; they signify the subject contents; for example in UDC the number 54 indicates a general document about chemistry. With each item classified like this, staff can organize books and other items on shelves in subject order so that users may browse.

A recent trend is for documents in electronic format to be linked to the catalogue, so that a hyperlink (an electronic reference) is provided allowing the user to view the document that has been indexed either on your organization's own computer or else via the internet – normally using a link to a website but it is possible to use links to remote file stores. This means that your users have a 'one stop shop' that allows them to identify and read documents from their screens, a trend that can only increase. Many of the documents retrieved will be either in a word processing format (typically Microsoft Word documents with a .doc extension) or in Portable Document Format, Adobe's proprietary format, which we also discuss elsewhere. Using these standard formats and ensuring that your local computers have the right software to read them will greatly improve your information centre's performance and accessibility.

Indexes and indexing

What does an index do?

An index will help the information seeker get hold of a piece of knowledge which is buried in the information service more quickly. An index will be found in print or computerized formats.

Where to find an index

There are various kinds of index. These are some places where you may expect to find one:

- at the back of a document, e.g. a book or report
- at the back of a list of standard specifications
- as a subject or author index to a list of journals
- as an alphabetical list of journal titles
- as a list of towns, cities or countries in an atlas or gazetteer.

How to make an index

In the simplest terms an index is made either manually, going through the document, or by using a computer, and picking out all the relevant important words. These are then arranged alphabetically, and have the page number on which they appear written alongside the word.

Creating a detailed index to a book or long report is a skilled task and you might consider contracting this out or finding out whether someone in your community has the necessary skills (perhaps a member of the Society of Indexers (**www.socind.demon.co.uk**)). Related items need to be linked together so that all sub-divisions are mentioned below the main heading, and there are links between the different names for the same idea. Some of the same principles apply as for making a catalogue, for example people's names are expressed as family name, given name. Some principles are peculiar to indexing, however; for example the linking of sub-headings within the entry – usually with a semi-colon – or the way page numbers are abbreviated in the listing.

Abstracts and abstracting

An abstract usually contains the salient points that can describe an article in a journal, or a document, book, conference paper and so on. There are three types of abstracts:

- indicative, which give the basic essential details that will identify the document
- informative, which give the basic essential details, plus keywords that more fully describe the article or document
- extensive, which give all the details of reference to the document, plus a longer abstract or summary, which could be 200–300 words, fully describing the document. Sometimes these extensive abstracts are so informative that it is not necessary to obtain the document itself because all the essential details are given, which can bring savings if you would otherwise have to borrow the item from another library.

How to make an abstract

To be able to make a successful abstract the information specialist will need to be able to transfer the details accurately, and be able to understand the document sufficiently well to be able to note down the full meaning of the text. If you or your staff do not have these skills, then you should consider taking on an external specialist, because if a document is not abstracted efficiently then the inaccurate abstract may mislead the information user.

Where to find an abstract

Many publications already contain an abstract or abstracts, often written by the author(s), which can be used without further work. Sometimes, however, it is better to take it and re-write or add more information that you know will help your own customers or readers.

There are also specialist journals that contain index entries or fuller abstracts for documents and other publications. The modern history of abstracting journals can be traced back at least 300 years so has a long tradition. However, the recent development of computer-based indexing and abstracting has revolutionized this tradition. Now many users prefer to consult an online database, which usually contains abstracts and can be extensively searched using powerful software.

How to build up a database

Once you have indexed your documents and provided abstracts or keywords, if appropriate, your database starts to build up. A personal computer equipped with suitable database management software will provide you with an effective means of managing it. You can use some common database packages such as Microsoft Access or Lotus Notes to build some remarkably sophisticated databases with search facilities and a well featured user interface, but there are a number of very useful, relatively cheap packages that will do a good job for you too. The user may add, modify or delete information and build up tailor-made databases. As we mentioned above, it is important to be consistent and we recommend that the database structure (data elements in the fields) should be reflected accurately in the form used to enter the data or in which the data is imported from other applications.

When selecting or configuring a database management system you should make sure that it allows you to carry out a number of key activities. You can build your own list by observing the way your information centre will operate, but we suggest that it should: retrieve records by any of the fields in their contents, either singly or in combination; display the records in full or part according to the criteria defined by the user; sort records into a given sequence defined by the user; and allow the user to print a partial or full catalogue and/or index entries for all records selected. It is also helpful if the search form shows all the fields present in the record so that users do not search for non-existent parts of the record, and it would also help them to know about the formats; for example, for dates, so that they know they have to search for, say, 01/04/05, not 04-01-2005.

Enquiry services

The information centre is your user's contact point to find detailed information on specific subjects. You will receive two types of enquiry: for a specific document, or for information on a given topic.

An information centre will need to decide what kind of 'extended services' it will offer customers inside the organization and externally. These may cover a wide range from delivering free publications to a full technical enquiry service, which could be offered as 'a value added service', where enquiries by e-mail, letter, fax, telephone or by personal visits are encouraged. These extended services could include giving talks or offering training courses. We discuss ways of promoting the centre and these various services in Chapter 7.

Loan services

In order to manage the loan of documents, the centre should have a set of standard forms (such as loan request forms, request form for journals, interlibrary loan request forms and date due cards). The items can be requested electronically or by telephone – sometimes sent by letter or on a form – but a database containing these request forms may be used for this purpose. Again there are software packages available that will help.

In the UK and many other countries you will need to ensure that you have a record of the request in a suitable format to demonstrate compliance with copyright law. The Copyright and Related Rights Regulations 2003 set the current requirements for libraries in the UK and placed additional constraints on copying for commercial purposes. We illustrate a typical copyright declaration form in Appendix 1, which you can adapt.

If you request articles from the British Library Document Supply Centre, you will find that they attach a similar copyright declaration form, which you should ask the requester to complete before you issue the document. You should then file the form as a record to demonstrate compliance, but do not send it back to the British Library.

You will need to decide what kind of loan service you will provide and what will be the timescale for a standard loan – perhaps two weeks, with maybe an extended loan service for users with particular need for extended use of an item, such as tutors leading a course.

You will need to have a recall system to retrieve items that may be required by other users or to remind users that they have had an item out on loan for more than the agreed period and that it is overdue. Allow users to renew items but insist on seeing them at intervals to ensure that they have not been lost. Fines are most commonly used in public libraries but it may be appropriate to charge overdue users in other situations, such as if you have had to pay charges to the BLDSC or other external body. You will need some sanctions to reclaim payment for missing items or unpaid fines; you could decide to suspend the library privileges of anyone who fails to pay what they owe, or to arrange for a claim to be sent to the accounts department if your centre serves employees of an organization.

Periodicals

What do we mean by these terms? The word 'periodical' is an inclusive term for all publications issued at (usually) regular intervals, each issue being numbered in sequence and dated. They may appear daily, weekly, monthly, quarterly or annually. Other terms used for periodicals are journals, magazines, newsletters, archives or series. Some examples of different types of periodicals are:

- daily newspapers
- general interest magazines
- learned, specialist journals
- trade journals
- foreign language journals
- societies' or associations' magazines containing news and articles for their members.

It is easier to treat some of these as special cases, for example newspapers and general interest magazines, which are often easier to order from local newsagents (for a small information centre) or through specialist suppliers who know the newspaper trade very thoroughly. It is important that these apparently simple items are delivered to time ('Who wants yesterday's papers?') – especially where, as with evening newspapers, there are several editions, which change during the day.

To save time when you order periodicals, magazines and newspapers for your information centre we recommend that you talk first to a subscription agent. This could save you time and money in the long run if your requirements are anything other than very simple. Although agents will probably charge for their services, this charge should be balanced by the discounts they can obtain for large purchases of individual titles. Elsewhere we discuss additional services such as 'consolidation', which involves the agent marking in the copies on his computer and putting circulation lists onto the issues before they are delivered to you. Ask agents to provide quotations for your requirements, in terms both of the titles that you want and the services you need your chosen agent to provide. But once you have made your selection, be aware that it is quite complicated to change to a new agent as publishers need to be informed (unless you are buying consolidation) and there is a risk that you will lose issues of the journals you subscribe to. You might have to explain this to your finance people to avoid having to tender and re-let the agreement every single year, although there are also restrictions in EU regulations on the length of contracts that can now be made.

For small centres who can do without the services of an agent, the following details should help.

Identifying and locating magazines

Estimates of the number of periodicals currently published worldwide range from 80,000 to 200,000 – and that number is growing. Several guides exist to help in identifying the one you want. The guides usually list alphabetically the title, any previous titles, an abbreviated title, the publisher's name and address, and the date of first publication. The guides also give the international standard serial number, the unique eight-digit number applied to each title, and they provide keywords or a description of the content and state the frequency of publication.

Among the best known directories are *Ulrich's International Periodicals Directory*, the *World List of Scientific Periodicals* and *Willings Press Guide*. These are available in printed form or as online databases, and can be useful in your information centre.

Recording magazines

When a magazine arrives at your office or information centre, it is important to keep a record of this fact and to note its receipt. If someone enquires about it later and it is missing, you will know whether it was received or not and so you won't have to hound the agent or supplier! Recording the date of receipt enables you to know if it arrives regularly and whether an issue is overdue. For this purpose make a record (whether this is an entry in an electronic database or on a card) for each magazine showing its title, frequency (for example, monthly), number of copies and how long you have decided to retain it (for example, two years).

The name of the supplier or agent is also needed in case you have to pursue missing copies. The receipt date of each issue should be noted on the card so that if a particular issue fails to arrive (and this is why it is important to record the exact issue numbers, as well as the volume) you can chase it up with the agent or supplier. You will notice that an issue is missing when the next one arrives and the previous one has not turned up. It is a good idea, especially with less frequent items, to make a regular check on receipt cards for long overdue magazines, as otherwise you may miss an issue. A month is the longest you should wait as a publisher only prints a limited number and may not be able to supply back numbers.

If you decide to use a manual system it may be possible to track down suitable pre-printed cards for the purpose, or you can use a word-processing package to create cards with a suitable layout. Software packages are also available, which ease the job of recording magazine receipts. If you use a subscription agent they will often be able to offer a package linked to their particular system or alternatively advise on the most appropriate.

Circulating magazines

If a magazine is of interest to various members of an organization, it is useful to keep a copy in the information centre for reference purposes. If, however, it is only of interest to a few it may be better to circulate it. Take the decision based on whether you believe you can be confident of finding the person who holds a magazine at any time that you need it.

After recording receipt on the appropriate card, a circulation slip should be attached listing the names of the people who wish to see it and, at the top of the list, the designation of the office where it will be retained permanently. To encourage prompt movement between readers they should be required to initial and date the circulation slip before they pass it on. The receipt card should include details of the circulation list. Examine magazines that return from circulation to see if anyone is obviously causing delays, and either move them down the list or ask whether they can circulate items more quickly.

An alternative to circulation is to photocopy the contents page when it arrives and send this instead of the magazine itself to interested parties; individuals can then ask for copies of articles they are interested in. You must make sure that you adhere to the copyright regulations in your country when you do this. By using this method you may be able to reduce the number of copies you purchase.

How long to keep magazines

The length of time during which you can justify keeping back numbers of a magazine, considering all the storage arrangements that this entails, should be given serious consideration. This may vary from a few months for a fairly ephemeral magazine to ten years for one that is frequently referred to. It is certainly not necessary to hang on to every magazine forever – and in any case there is probably not enough space to do so. When deciding on the retention period, ask yourself the following questions:

- How much is the magazine used? Is it constantly in demand? Is it only the current issue that is of interest? For example, if it is a newsy magazine that is interesting in the short term but does not contain substantial articles to be referred to in later years, it should be kept for a short time, perhaps one year only.
- Does your local public library keep back issues? Ask whether they will lend magazines and make your policy accordingly.
- The British Library Document Supply Centre holds a wide range of magazines, so if you only get an occasional request for back issues,

consider throwing out some of your older copies and borrowing from them (or another document supplier) as necessary.

- Last, but not least, how much space have you got for storage? Some people still prefer to bind issues together, but this can be costly, so if you do keep a back run, it should probably be as single issues. Make a note on the receipt card of the period during which that particular magazine is to be retained and be rigorous about throwing out those outside the retention period.

Magazine storage

All magazine issues should be kept together either in neat piles on shelves, with the most recent issue on top, or in labelled boxes. You can obtain these boxes from specialist library suppliers although you can also find them in stationery shops. If you are keeping magazines for a long time, ensure that you have good quality boxes – if they are certified as 'archival quality' you should be confident that they will not damage the contents through poor materials.

Filing magazines

Keep magazines in alphabetical order by title and label the box or the edge of the shelf with appropriate titles. You can use abbreviations if necessary. You can use embossed plastic tape for labelling shelf edges, or label makers are available fairly cheaply to print on adhesive paper.

Lists of magazines

It is useful to have a list of magazines to which you subscribe. It should show the titles you take, the frequency of publication and record the length of time you retain back copies. It is useful for new members of your organization to tell them what you hold, as well as for answering enquiries from occasional customers of your service.

We saw earlier that indexes to books are arranged by the name of the author, but periodicals are arranged by title.

Enquiries

To answer questions consistently about a given subject, you must have a strategy. This task may be simplified by dividing it into the following stages:

- Clarify the question by checking the enquirer's existing information.
- Search appropriate sources for the information that answers the enquiry. After ensuring that the information which you have found is validated and authoritative, interpret it into a form suitable for the enquirer.
- Present your findings in a professional manner; list the question, sources used and answers given. You can present these electronically by e-mail or send them on paper. Ask your enquirer whether they have a preferred format.

Keep a log of your enquiries and the answers given. This is useful for statistical and qualitative purposes and also for if there is any comeback from your enquirer. It may be that you can identify some frequently asked questions that can be added to your library website, but take care to check that the answers are updated frequently so that they remain accurate.

It is essential to clarify exactly what the question is at the outset. This essentially means focusing on the underlying purpose of the customer's question – not so much what they actually asked, but what they wanted to know or intended to ask. Sometimes users will try to help you by doing what they think is part of your work themselves. Thus they might want to know about the amount of recycling that happens each year but will ask for information about council services, which could lead to their being given a much broader and unhelpful answer than the one they want. Probe to discover the exact question that needs answering and pay attention to accuracy. These two steps will help to ensure that you provide what is actually required and avoid any problems that might occur from the use of incorrect information. Only use validated and authoritative sources when you are answering enquiries; there is a lot of unsubstantiated information on the internet for example, which could be positively dangerous to use in some situations.

Contacts and sources

When reviewing sources and methods for retrieval of information it is very important that you do not restrict yourself to computer-based information, and so neglect the more traditional manual sources. It can be quicker to search manually to answer simple urgent enquiries than to use databases or the internet, which throws up a lot of unwanted extra information that has to be sifted and discarded. Think how much detail is really needed to answer the enquiry and do not swamp the user if all they need is a simple answer.

Send the answer to the enquirer by the fastest appropriate method. It helps the user to know how the information was collected, so even if a reply is sent by e-mail, it can include this detail. However you send the information, ensure that it is understandable, well organized and well presented, so that it will reflect the high standard of work and effort that you put into investigating the enquiry.

Reference collections

Most information centres will need collections for self service and staff use in dealing with common enquiries or reference enquiries – that is, those that can be answered by a collection of reference books – such as telephone and trade directories, or annual reference books like *Who's Who*. Reference services offer quick information face-to-face, by telephone or e-mail. They can also gather files of information for special groups or on specific topics; and they prepare abstracts and literature summaries. Other activities could include instruction sessions to help users become more effective and efficient in the use of the reference resources and helping them to develop their skills so they can search information resources independently.

Disseminating information

Internally

You can disseminate information to your internal users either by supplying them with the information they need ('push') or by giving them the opportunity to gain access to it ('pull'). A library bulletin is an example of 'push', with subscribers receiving a regular list of new materials, items of interest, and so on. If the list is published to an information centre website for readers to access as and when they wish, we consider this as 'pull' – in other words we may choose to push information to our users when we want to make sure they read it, or allow them to pull data when they remember or want it. Although 'push' is still considered a better marketing tool than 'pull' by many writers, you need to make sure that it does not become intrusive and lead people to unsubscribe from your services. 'Push' has been a particular success where websites have been set up to send news bulletins to subscribers when new regulations or guidance have been issued in their fields.

Externally

There will often be external interest in your bulletin, especially if yours is a specialist subject area. You will need to decide whether external subscribers will be allowed to have access (there may be security concerns for example) and whether they should be asked to pay for copies. Remember that if you have specialist materials this may lead to demand to lend items to external borrowers, which will mean your core clients lose access while the items are away. Make sure that everyone, including your managers and suppliers of funds, understands your policies and how you arrived at them. Keep statistics of use and review the situation regularly. Some centres find that having subscribing members from a defined external community both assures them of an income and ensures that the specialists in their field are aware of their services.

Translation and interpreting services

Sometimes the information centre may be required to organize translations or interpretation services. If this is so, ensure that you hold details of organizations or individuals who can offer such a service, especially if they are local to you or have good response times. There are a number of services available which will be able to provide quality translation and interpreting with subject specialization. Depending on your subject area translation may be an important element, for example in making scientific information in Russian or Japanese available to your users. Poor translation services will reflect poorly on your service if you are the primary link to them.

Standards and response times

As part of your service quality programme you should have some standards of service and response times that will help information services staff and users to know what is expected. For example you could adopt guidelines like those shown in Table 6.1.

Table 6.1 Expected response time for different services

Service	Expected response time (turnaround time)
1. Answering loan requests	a) 3 days for 80% of requests
	b) longer for remaining 20% – user to be informed
2. Making photocopies	a) 2 days for 80% of requests
	b) longer for remaining 20%
3. Ordering loans/document supply from external source	a) within 24 hours, urgent action for 10%
	b) 10–15 days for 80%
	c) in excess of 20 days for remaining 10%
4. Carrying out an extensive literature search	a) 1–10 days for 80%
	b) 11–20 days for 10%
	c) longer for remaining 10%, depends on the nature of the enquiry
5. Making translations	a) within 48 hours if urgent – for 10%
	b) normal – negotiable between panels of linguists and staff turnaround – 90% of requests
6. Ordering new items for stock	a) up to 8 weeks for 70% of requests
	b) 8 weeks and over if from other parts of the world
	c) exceptions, e.g. British Standards, within 36 hours
7. Entering a new stock item into database	a) up to 10 working days for 70%
	b) over 10 working days for 30%
8. Answering telephone calls or e-mail messages	a) same day if no research is needed; if not above applies

Other services tailored to particular user groups

Always keep in mind whether further services can be supplied, for example if frequent enquiries on the same subject suggest that a new SDI service – Selective Dissemination of Information – could be offered on that particular subject. You may be able to do this by adapting (or dropping) existing services but the final decision will probably be dictated by issues like the number of staff you have and their particular knowledge or skills. It could be worthwhile keeping needs in mind when recruiting new staff (what languages do they speak? What subjects have they studied?), and you may be able to offer new services based on their skills. However, bear in mind that there is an associated risk if those people leave your organization, as the service may then have to close even if it has been very popular, or you will have to investigate buying it in for the future.

It makes sense for these services to be developed by the information centre. Many organizations waste money and time by obtaining multiple copies of the same information and it is here that the information service can have enormous effect. Organizations need to be reminded that there are many sources of information, but not all of them can be trusted. Information service staff must get over the message loud and clear that information is certainly not all free and on the internet! Library and information professionals have a special role to play, putting users in touch with information and providing a range of services to support that role. The skills of library and information professionals are needed in many organizations, and the information centres they create are a valuable resource.

Summary

In this chapter we have looked at:

- the variety of services that can be offered
- what steps to take in setting up the services
- other types of help from outside suppliers
- how to organize information
- indexes and indexing, abstracts and abstracting
- how to build up a database
- types of enquiry services
- what a reference collection is
- loan and photocopying services

- different ways to disseminate information
- translation and interpreting services
- other services tailored to particular user groups.

7

Support for the library and information service

• •

In this chapter we examine the various means of support that may be available for your centre. These include:

- management support
- financial support
- organizational support
- technical support
- network support
- external support.

• •

Management support

Starting a service from scratch is always going to be an uphill struggle without support and endorsement within your community or organization. Therefore if you have the support of management, or better still a management champion, your new service will be put at an advantage.

What might this management support consist of? First of all, we should identify who could provide it, so that we can see what kind of support could be forthcoming. In a business or an existing public sector body the management role is pretty clear – it's a person who is more senior than the information service manager and to whom that manager reports. In a community it's a senior person who has influence or some other kind of central position, such as a head teacher or deputy, or perhaps someone who sits on the board of a learned society or professional college. Whoever it is, the characteristics of that person will include their position of influence or authority, and usually their seniority to the information service manager. It makes some difference whether they are directly responsible for managing the information service manager, since that will affect their ability to instruct the manager to carry out particular tasks or offer particular services, or merely pass back suggestions and comments from others. Being the information service manager's direct boss will also affect the degree of shared interest that the person will have in the success of the information centre so far as their own performance goes.

We hope that support from your manager (whoever it is) is interested rather than dutiful, and reflects a genuine wish to be responsible for your service rather than an 'Oh dear, I've been given the library' kind of attitude. But either sort of manager should be pleased to be responsible for the people and place that provide so many members of any organization or community with one of their consistently positive experiences. Keep copies of the compliments that the service receives, and report on them at regular intervals, for example in your monthly or other regular report to management. Many surveys show how well the users of library and information services regard these reports and the people who provide them; take advantage by surveying your users (even if they send you unsolicited testimonials!) and by presenting the results to your management. Managers should soon realize what a treasure they are indirectly responsible for. Remind them to tell others about the facilities and services that you offer and keep them aware of your achievements. Also emphasize how useful the information service can be in other projects that may be taking place with the organization.

Non-specialist managers are notoriously unaware of what library and information services do, and need to be shown. We hope that you get regular time with whoever manages your particular community – if not, ask whether you can meet regularly and keep them up to date with what is going on. Pitch what you say to their needs, not exclusively your own. Think how your service fits into their agenda, so that you can give them news and information that they can use in turn when somebody more senior asks: 'What goes on in that library or information centre?'

We think that managers should:

* take the time to understand what it is you and your team do
* understand why they should be the ones to do it

- provide regular feedback on what the organization or community is doing so that you can tailor services to the needs that those activities create
- provide support up the line that comes from an informed interest (beware the manager who says, 'X says this about you, how do I respond to that?' and develop their understanding as fast as you can)
- give a commitment to take your good news stories to the wider audience of movers and shakers in your community.

Your side of the deal is to be professional at all times, and to do your best for your community and your manager as part of that professionalism.

Financial support

What financial support does your community provide for you, and how is it managed? Whether you work for a public body or a private one, there will be some kind of financial structure within which you must work. If you are in a fee-collecting organization of some sort, you may even be faced with a situation where you must price your services in order to cover salaries, cost of materials and perhaps the cost of accommodation, light, heat and so on. Most organizations do this by working out what money they have and what they will spend over a period of one financial year (which may be the calendar year or some other 12-month period such as April to March to coincide with the fiscal or tax year).

If the situation is reasonably straightforward, you will receive a sum of money each year that is supposed to provide for your expected costs. You are almost certain to have to account for this, and even if this function is carried out centrally you would be well advised to keep some sort of record (which might be in your library housekeeping system) to tell you how much you have spent, because bills are not always paid straight away by finance departments, so you could appear to have more funds remaining than is actually the case.

Annual expenditure

It is not too difficult to make the system predict how much you will have spent at the end of the year, as if you provide details of your subscriptions and other major items of expenditure, the remainder can be distributed over the financial accounting year to provide estimated targets for your spend. Table 7.1 shows how this might work for you in a year running from 1 April to 31 March.

Table 7.1 Monthly spend for a budget of £12,000 a year, distributed evenly

Month	Apr	May	Jun	Jul	Aug	Sep	Oct	Nov	Dec	Jan	Feb	Mar
£	1000	1000	1000	1000	1000	1000	1000	1000	1000	1000	1000	1000

Now look at what happens when you adjust this 'flat' profile to take into account the times when you know you will have larger invoices to pay. Table 7.2 shows the monthly spend for a budget of £12,000 a year, allowing for standing orders renewal in April, new course materials in September, subscription renewals in December, end-of-year purchase of optional titles in February, and low spend in August (due to holidays) and March (due to end of financial year).

Table 7.2 Monthly spend for a budget of £12,000 a year, allowing for various adjustments

Month	Apr	May	Jun	Jul	Aug	Sep	Oct	Nov	Dec	Jan	Feb	Mar
£	2000	500	500	500	250	1500	500	500	3000	500	2000	250

The obvious difference between these two patterns is that in Table 7.2 the spending is much more uneven. But it is also realistic, so that when the bill for £3000 of subscriptions arrives in December it will not cause panic because it exceeds the monthly average (as in the flat profile) by £2000.

Work out what pattern of spending suits you, and decide how much variation you will allow from it. Do this as a percentage, because in the second example above a bill for £500 will blow the budget in August or March, whereas in the flat profile it will not – even though it disguises a potential problem because the bill is much larger than you were predicting for that time of the financial year. Update your plans at intervals throughout the year to make sure they are on target.

Using a spreadsheet

If you are adept at using spreadsheets, convert the table into a graph so that you can see how spending should vary each month (see Figure 7.1). If you

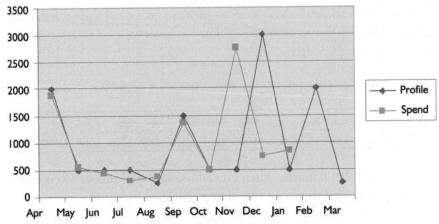

Figure 7.1 The figures shown in Table 7.2 in graph form

plot a second line that shows how much you have spent, you can see at once how you are performing against your targets. In the chart below, you can see that although the main bill was presented and paid a month early, the spend is close to the profile so the information centre's finance manager can be confident about being able to meet the second big bill in February. (In fact, the spend is only £5 off the profile in the sample used, so the manager deserves congratulation!)

Make use of those with expertise

You may be lucky enough – or unlucky if you consider it is too controlling – to have your finances monitored and managed centrally. Maybe there is a team who pay invoices for you, or prepare financial forecasts. Talk to them and get to know them, so that you know you can call on their help if there are problems to solve rather than having them take you in for questioning when things go wrong! They may well provide you with records of spending that will save you considerable work, although we would still advise you not to rely entirely on their records unless you are certain that they are up to date and capable of reflecting the way that library suppliers and the book trade work. Information professionals often have a difficult time explaining why they appear to be underspending for months on end when in fact they are simply ensuring that there are sufficient funds to pay for all the subscriptions when the bills arrive relatively late in the financial year. The flat profile model shown in Table 7.1 does you no favours in this kind of regime.

Look for sources of funding that can provide you with financial support. If you generate income, let the community know. It may be that you have regular users who are prepared to contribute the cost of the service you provide to them, or else that there are funds that can help. Whatever the position, ensure that you are in command of the financial situation. Know the true costs you incur: printed information materials usually have delivery costs attached; electronic information has sales or value added tax added to the cost in many countries; the cost of employing somebody is far higher than their salary costs because of employer taxes; premises are not free of charge, because somebody has to heat and light them, keep them clean and pay property tax. We provide sources of help on this in the reading list.

Library finance can sometimes be tricky but it should not be difficult if you are methodical and keep your wits about you. If you need to deal with a central finance team in your organization or community, try to show them that you know what you are doing. Financial managers are wary of libraries because their invoice patterns appear unpredictable, so be ready to show that you understand their concerns. Have an explanation ready to show how annual invoices for serials are in fact predictable, and that you are ready for them. Explain simply what standing orders are and how your calculations allow for them. If the finance people are not worried about you, and if you send in dependable returns on time, they will probably adopt a light touch approach and leave you alone – unless you want to ask for help on any topic.

The key message here is that you are not alone. Although it helps if you are numerate, you are not expected to be a financial genius who could get a job as a city dealer. There are financial experts in many organizations just as you are their information and library specialist, and you should use their services in the same way that you want them to use yours. Legal and professional compliance is very important in many situations and you should not try to do without the services of a profession whose work you do not fully understand.

Organizational support

What help can other people provide for you within your organization or community? Who are your internal supporters? How much help will the infrastructure of your workplace give you in creating a high quality service?

Information services often benefit from the good will they create through their excellent services. This is something that you may not actually exploit (you might think that was a bit too Machiavellian) but certainly something that can help you. People will often recognize the contribution that the service makes, will probably be interested if you have plans or issues that you want to discuss, and may well be prepared to speak up for you. (But don't expect them to hand over chunks of their own budget if times are tight!) You could find that your service creates its own champions across the community – people you can keep in touch with for ideas and support. It may be worth forming them into some kind of panel or committee that you can meet from time to time to tell them about your progress and to gather ideas from. What kind of new services do they want you to provide? What doesn't warrant the effort that you are putting into it?

Identify supporters by making sure you are represented at events in your community and using these opportunities to get your activities noticed. Develop your 'lift speech', so called because it contains the few sentences that you will memorize as an answer to the question 'What does your team do?' if you end up alone in the lift with an influential member of the community.

Networking and some other kinds of support can be helpful within your community or organization, and we come to these very shortly.

Technical support

Many library and information professionals have strong technical skills. This has been recognized through the creation of 'converged' library teams, where librarians who have learned IT skills are joined by IT people who have learned basic library and information skills. In this way the team can operate a service to agreed quality standards over a longer working day, knowing that its members can cover all the basic tasks, whether information management or information technology related.

However, in many situations basic IT skills are not enough and you will need support. Many information service operations rely on the availability of IT that is not under the direct control of the staff. The people who operate and manage this IT must become your friends! There may well be times when they are not available to you – services may well fail when the information service is the only part of the organization that is working, such as at weekends – but you may still be able to obtain some kind of support from them. You may need to reassure the IT team that your library management software will not bring down their entire system. This could mean asking your suppliers to talk to them in their own language, but it's worth doing if necessary. Be clear about what your suppliers are contracted to do, and also ask who they are contracted to, as in some organizations it will be the IT department or even the finance department, but not you. Some suppliers prefer to liaise with the information service, and it would be a good idea to talk to your suppliers about the way they like to work before it becomes necessary to discover that while you deal with a crisis.

Network support

Sometimes you will need someone to talk through a problem with, and sometimes you will want some formal advice. One of the things that makes the library and information profession so special is that way that people network between organizations, between sectors and even between countries. Joining professional networks will give you a source of support that will help you through many situations, and may give you the opportunity of repaying that support to your colleagues.

There are a number of professional organizations that provide opportunities to network. Most obvious are the national professional bodies such as CILIP in the UK, but there are many others for particular sectors or types of information work. Sub-groups or special interest groups of the national bodies fulfil this role, as well as some independent groups. All of them rely to a considerable extent on input from volunteer members of their committees and working groups. Although there will clearly be some demands on your time if you decide to take an active part in the work of these bodies, you will probably find that your contribution is repaid with interest by the contacts you make and the support they can give you. You may even find that your community is willing to give you time for this networking as part of your own professional development, and it's worth asking, but it is more common to work on committees where members invest their own time and effort because of what they get in return.

External support

Organizations of friends and supporters

A considerable number of libraries and information services have supporters' organizations or 'friends of the library' groups that help them in a number of tangible and intangible ways. Often they exist because the information service is under-resourced and can benefit from fund-raising activities that it is not permitted to run directly for itself. The friends organization is not bound by the same rules and is able to carry out these activities and pass the proceeds to the library. This can certainly provide a welcome addition to the resources of the smaller information service, while for larger organizations the friends can act as a kind of independent advisory committee. But you need to keep in mind that friends and supporters will have a particular view on issues concerned with the way the library is run that will not always align with what you or your managers think.

Professional bodies

The national and specialist professional bodies will give you valuable support in starting your service from scratch. Although they will not be able to do the job for you they will provide contacts for many of the activities we describe in this book, and their special interest groups will put you in touch with other professionals working in your subject and geographic area.

Smaller specialist groups

You may also discover that there are local networks that can provide you with practical support from others in similar positions to yourself. These can range from 'one-person-band' clubs to associations of local colleges or schools. Many will time their meetings to take account of the fact that you have a day job and that you cannot easily take time off for meetings by closing the centre. If you are willing to use some of your free time (or negotiate some compensatory time off) then these groups can be particularly valuable as their members will be facing situations like your own. If the members are from private companies they will have a code of ethics, like not discussing details of their businesses, but they will still be able to offer helpful support. It can be difficult to track down these groups when they are local in nature, but a few enquiries will often find them. The local public library may know about them, for example, or a web search will turn up a link. You could even take a proactive approach and contact others in similar types of community or organization to see if they are interested, or as we suggest above you could attend a local meeting of a branch of CILIP (or whatever your national professional body is) to see who is there.

Summary

This chapter has shown that although setting up an information centre can be a major task, you can always find support even when you are a one-person team. We have included an overview of financial management, which is an essential skill, to show that you can do many basic tasks yourself – knowing what you can and cannot do will assist you in judging when to ask for help. We have also looked at various internal and external networks that you can tap into. If none of these provide what you are looking for, you can use your information skills to locate possible contacts, with a view to starting your own support network. Your counterparts in other organizations may well welcome the approach, so don't be shy if this appears to be the best way forward!

8

Promoting the library and information service

• •
In this chapter we look at the opportunities to promote your library and information service. We consider:

- different types of promotional activity
- how to target activities
- hints and tips for each activity
- assessing the impact of each type of activity.
• •

In order to establish the library and information service or centre as a resource within the community you will need to promote the various activities in which it will be involved and the services and benefits that it can provide. This is important whether you work in the public, private, academic or voluntary sector, and can be done in various ways. Some of these are virtually cost-free while others involve some expense, and for some you will need help from other experts.

In the sections below we look at the following activities and types of promotion:

- advertising in general
- press releases
- writing articles or information notes for the trade and technical press
- organizing visits to the LIS for interested parties
- participating in seminars, conferences and exhibitions
- publications, including information sheets or leaflets – free and priced
- publicity packages

- creating a union list of journals
- information centre newsletters
- seminars and training courses

Advertising
In journals

In the information centre's plan of work you may need to have part of the budget funds allocated to advertising costs if free publicity is not an option. We shall look below at how to place advertisements cost effectively. You should aim to make use of journals produced in the locality or covering the subject area in which the centre is promoting itself. Select a size that will have the necessary impact in comparison with other advertisements, but allow you to keep within budgetary limits. Space is sold either as a fraction of a page (full, half, quarter, and so on) or as column centimetres. The advertising manager of each publication will be able to provide a rate card showing charges and copy dates, and a number of journals publish this information in their advertisement pages. If a multi-publication campaign is envisaged, an advertising agency may be able to save you time and money by having suitable contacts and by advising on ways to reach your audience in the most effective ways.

In your own publications

Your own publications provide you with an opportunity to advertise your centre and its services. Every publication that is issued from the library or information centre should include:

- the full name of the organization
- your contact details
- a brief (one-line) statement of the purpose of the centre to ensure that there is a periodic reminder to all who receive its material of its existence and the services that it can provide.

Press releases

Why promote the information centre using press releases?

Your centre should aim to remain in the public eye by continuous promotion of its role and services. Press releases allow you to issue regular updates with details of the centre's current activities. The editors of trade and technical publications are always anxious to have up-to-date news on new developments: for example:

- an announcement of a new issue of the centre's bulletin or newsletter
- details of any new leaflets issued
- news of additional services such as the setting up of an enquiry service
- an announcement of new legislation or revision of a piece of legislation
- an announcement of a new publicity campaign or special event
- news about conferences and training courses
- an announcement of a new list of publications
- news of the appointment of new staff
- the announcement that your annual statistics have been issued.

What goes into a press release?

Each press release must contain:

- the name and address of the organization issuing it
- the date of the press release
- the number of the press release (using a running number either from a set reserved for your information centre or taken from the parent organization's sequence).

The main body of the text must be written succinctly and contain the main points of the message in the first paragraph as this will probably be quoted exactly elsewhere. This information is usually contained in one or two pages. If there are a number of pages carrying particular information, such as statistics, then these can be added as an appendix.

Press releases are aimed initially at editors or the media, and many releases have a separate part called 'notes for editors' to provide additional background information and more details. Be brief and to the point –

remember the people you are addressing are busy people and you are dependent on their good will. You are also competing with many other press releases received daily by the editor.

Consider the type of publication you are writing for. There are a number of books about journalistic style that will guide you. Keep the ideas simple and straightforward, and write for the lay person unless you are sure that the audience will understand any technical or specialist issues. Compare the styles used by publications such as your house journal (if you work in a corporate organization), your local newspaper, specialist publications for the library and information profession, and the 'red top' tabloids and the 'heavy' newspapers (what were until recently the broadsheets).

Spell out any initials or acronyms used in the press release especially if it is being sent to editors of journals or people in the media who may wish to expand on the details given.

Who should receive press releases?

As we suggested above, editors of relevant journals, newspapers and newsletters should all receive copies of press releases. It would be useful to compile a list of the editors of key publications in your area with their names and contact details so that labels for envelopes can be made and the press releases sent out efficiently. Radio and TV news and feature programmes may also want to run a story about your service so their news-desk editors should also be sent your press releases. Staff working on specialist publications may only wish to receive press releases relating to their specialist subjects, so arrangements should be made for them in this case. You should also send your press releases to local associations, societies and other organizations who may want to make use of your services. A press release will provide the editors of their publications with the opportunity to describe your services with an eye to their members' interests, and to use the contact details you provide to ask for further details that their members may want to know.

Another way of promotion is to make the press releases available on your website or via e-mail. There is a lot of interest in sites that send news releases by e-mail to people who have registered their wish to receive up-to-date information, and providing this service helps you to target your news to an audience you know is receptive.

We have provided a sample press release in Appendix 3. You can readily find examples of the press releases of other established centres on the web (see for example the site of the British Library), or you could ask some of these organizations for sample releases.

Writing articles

Editors of newspapers and the media in general are keen to receive articles describing centre activities, publications and services. We suggest that every centre should 'cultivate' editors who may provide opportunities for free publicity.

Although the trade press is an increasingly professional business, and even newsletters of professional interest groups are written to an incredibly high standard, there is still room for 'inspired' articles that tell the profession about your achievements. Contact the editor of the journal or newsletter that covers your field to see if they or a reporter will come to talk to you. You may need to insist that you see the copy for comment, especially if you work in an organization that has a press office which needs to vet copy about your company or organization before it appears in print. But most editors are happy to allow this provided that you do not take away their editorial independence (so limit the 'party line' that you press).

General publications may also be willing to take copy from you, if it is tailored to their audience. Local newspapers may pick up on your centre's achievements from other sources and call on you if they become aware that something newsworthy has happened in your organization. If some good fortune comes your way why not practise your 'lift speech' – the one that explains in 45 seconds (the time between the ground floor and the management floor in the lift) what is so special and important about your centre, so that you can convince a journalist that you have a story worth telling to a wider audience.

Organizing visits to the centre

Information centres are still a place of mystery to many potentials users so a chance to see behind the scenes may be welcome. Such visits give you a chance to explain to users and potential users what goes on, and what services are available. Many surveys show that people love their libraries and are great supporters of them – but they don't use all the services available and base their views only on the services they use. Think how much more enthusiastic people might be if they know about all your services and which ones are useful to them! Visits to the centre (open days or regular visits at a given time each week) provide you with a way to approach users.

As an example, one information centre announced in an article in its in-house journal that it would be hosting visits in order to make information seekers, internal and external, aware of the range of information produced and stored at the centre. Interested groups of potential visitors included specialists, students, various associations, and trade union representatives as well as many others. (See below some advice about organizing seminars and training courses.)

Participating in conferences, seminars and exhibitions

One well-tried way of making individuals and organizations aware of the existence of an information centre is for the head of the centre to be available as a public speaker. The head of centre may need to attend a course on public speaking, which will show how to prepare and deliver a talk, organize notes, produce a PowerPoint presentation, operate a projector and answer questions from the audience. Alternatively a number of films and videos are available on public speaking (although you learn a great deal by just doing it). Many conferences are run in parallel with an exhibition. Use the opportunity that such exhibitions offer to advertise the centre services. Even if the exhibition is run by a major conference organizer, there is often a joint stand for the use of smaller organizations where literature can be left and where the job of running the stand is shared between the exhibitors rather than you having to provide someone to stay there throughout the exhibition.

Public speaking

You don't have to be a gifted orator in order to give an effective talk to either a small informal group, or a large public gathering. There is a difference between lecturing and public speaking, where you have to be able to hold an audience. The principal requirements for public speaking are having a sound knowledge of the subject, self-confidence and some practical experience of giving a talk. A number of texts exist on the subject, but here are our tips:

- Speakers' appearance, voice, dress and mannerisms will be the focal point for the audience. Audiences will react to appearance, and their response can condition their minds to accept or reject the talk before the speaker even starts. Take care, therefore, about the way you present yourself.
- Tell your audience what subject(s) are to be covered, and what are the main points to be covered. Then cover all these points and conclude with a summary of the main points. This all sounds very simple and mechanical, but it isn't. Remember that unless you present your key messages three times they are unlikely to be remembered.
- Use visual aids correctly. Do not talk to the screen but talk to the audience.
- Tell the audience that you will provide handouts after the talk; it is better not to give them out beforehand. Unless it's important that people in the audience can write additional notes, be aware that they will spend their time reading the notes and not listening to you.
- Decide whether you will answer questions during or at the end of the talk, and tell the audience at the beginning of the talk.
- Finally, if you are going to include a demonstration of a service, make sure that the person doing it is competent. Don't underestimate your audience's intelligence or skills. One of the authors remembers an occasion when a demonstrator tried to bluff his way through a demonstration to a senior manager without knowing that she had previously been a computing consultant! The result was of course embarrassing for all concerned, and it detracted from the message that was being put across about the professionalism of the centre.

Publications

A variety of types of publication offer opportunities to say more about your information centre.

Free leaflets

As the range of services develops there will be opportunities for the staff to produce leaflets on a range of subjects for issue free of charge to information seekers, for example, describing the work and services of the information centre.

Leaflet describing the work of the centre

These can be produced in-house or sent to a printing service to be issued as a glossy brochure. Discuss the number of copies to be printed, remembering that a longer print run in your initial order usually works out cheaper than having to send repeat orders. Typically, a library or information centre brochure will give:

- the name of the centre and full contact details
- opening times and a map showing the location of the centre
- a statement about who the centre belongs to
- a mission statement (see also Chapter 3)
- identity of the customers of the centre (i.e. who the service is available to both internally and externally)
- services provided, such as enquiry services, loans and photocopies, computerized services – including access to databases, electronic journals and CD-ROMs – the quick reference collection and publications such as journals and reports.

Leaflets describing specific work

We also suggest issuing leaflets about specific work. You could produce similar-looking small leaflets about each activity. Users may find that a document of perhaps four to six pages in length will explain everything to them, although leaflets can equally be on one side of an A4 sheet and may be more effective for your audience if you can make them so succinct. Aimed at giving the main points on a subject, they are usually written by experts to inform the users about individual services, so one might describe legislation available from the centre, and another the range of online services available to the users.

We recommend that centres start producing information sheets as early as possible in their existence as they are a proven, cost-effective way of improving the dissemination of practical information, and also function as an advertisement.

Many libraries and information centres will willingly send packs of their own leaflets to other centres, or at least do not mind if you visit them and collect samples of their publicity. Ask and perhaps save yourself valuable time and money as they may give you some ideas. There are no prizes for reinventing the wheel.

Things to consider when compiling a publication

Ask youself these questions when producing publicity material:

- **Why** are you producing this publicity?
- **What** message do you want to give?
- **Who** do you want to be able to understand your message?
- **When** do you want to use the publicity?
- **How often** do you want to update it?
- **How** will it be produced – is there a designer available?
- **How** will it be produced – can you afford to print it?
- **How** will you distribute it?
- **What** other details are needed? (Supply them!)

Publicity packages

Publicity packages are typically produced in a folder containing examples of the centre's newsletter, information about the centre and some of the small, specialized leaflets described above. As a next step, detail taken from these leaflets could be used to compile a useful composite promotional brochure for the centre. This brochure would give the contact details and state the centre's aims and objectives, services, publications and opening times. It could be updated with loose-leaf sheets about specific future events.

Examples are given in Appendix 4.

You can circulate these brochures in a variety of circumstances and formats:

- during publicity campaigns
- when answering enquiries, either in envelopes or attached in electronic format to e-mails (in modern IT systems prefer a hyperlink to the brochure on your intranet)

- as loose inserts in newsletters
- during training seminars and conferences
- as displayed material for visitors to the centre or others in the parent organization to take them away with them
- in electronic form on the centre's website.

Creating a union list of periodicals

The information centre can create useful publicity in academic and other research environments by creating a union list of periodicals that are held in libraries and information services in colleges, universities and other organizations in the locality. Knowledge of the locations of the periodicals will help the information seeker to access up-to-date information quickly.

How to compile a union list

1 First make a list of periodicals that are held or currently taken within the centre, using the titles printed on the cover of the periodical. Some periodical titles are artistically arranged, so if the title is in English read from the top left hand corner of the cover page and write the title as it is laid out.
2 Add the first dates of the periodical issues held in the centre, for example
        Safety and Health at Work, 1988–
3 Put the list into alphabetical order of titles, ignoring 'a', 'an', 'the', 'la', 'le' and so on.
4 Once the list is complete send it with a letter to other organizations asking if they would be willing to add their titles to the list; and also ask if individuals and organizations outside their own would be permitted to request photocopies of articles from them, or even visit them to carry out research using their periodicals.
5 If these organizations are willing to co-operate, add the name of the relevant contact person and organization, telephone and fax numbers to the union list.
6 Each of these organizations will be assigned a code, and their code number and holding dates of their journal titles will be added to the list. See the example in Figure 8.1.
    The third part of the union list could be the names of the organizations appearing in alphabetical order; see Figure 8.2.

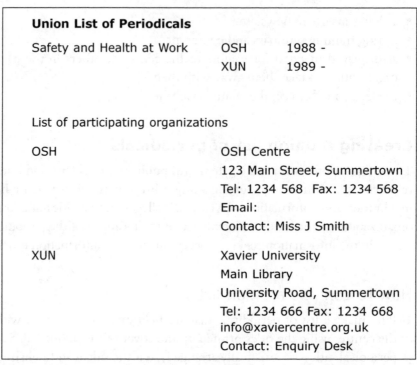

Union List of Periodicals

Safety and Health at Work   OSH   1988 -

XUN   1989 -

List of participating organizations

OSH

OSH Centre
123 Main Street, Summertown
Tel: 1234 568 Fax: 1234 568
Email:
Contact: Miss J Smith

XUN

Xavier University
Main Library
University Road, Summertown
Tel: 1234 666 Fax: 1234 668
info@xaviercentre.org.uk
Contact: Enquiry Desk

Figure 8.1 Use of codes in a union list of periodicals

Name of organization	Code number of organization
OSH Centre	OSH
123 Main Street	
Summertown	
Tel: 1234 568	
Fax: 1234 568	
Contact: Miss J Smith	
Xavier University	XUN
Main Library	
University Road	
Summertown	
Tel: 1234 666	
Fax: 1234 668	
Contact: Enquiry Desk	

Figure 8.2 The names of organizations in a union list of periodicals

The fourth part of a union list could be a subject index to the titles in the first part of the list. Each title needs to be classified from its contents. A simple, standard list of subject headings is recommended, to help avoid duplication.

Write or e-mail to established centres to ask for a copy of their subject listing for periodicals. An example is shown in Figure 8.3.

SUBJECT

Building and Construction
Construction Industry International
Safety and Health at Work
Site Safe News

Occupational Health
Adamstown Newsletter
CIS Newsletter
Safety and Health at Work

Figure 8.3 A subject listing in a union list of periodicals

7 The union list can be quite small in the beginning – containing perhaps only 100 or so titles – but in time it will grow as the centre and others include new titles. Some organizations may also wish to include CD-ROM or electronic titles held on the union list, in which case you need to include details about the availability of these titles to non-members of the organization in case licensing restrictions prevent external users from having access.

8 The list should be kept up to date. Either issue a new edition annually or send out a supplementary update sheet with additions and deletions. The list can be kept on a computer. The cover should give the name of the centre and contact details.

9 Copies of the union list should be distributed to all participating organizations and can also be made available to other appropriate organizations or individuals to encourage them to use the centre.

10 Issue a press release when the idea is launched to get other organizations interested – and do it again when the list is completed, or subsequently updated.

The information centre newsletter and website

The library or information centre's own newsletter and website should be the main channels for issuing information about the centre and its activities. They should contain current news and activities of the centre, promoting the services that it provides, highlighting training opportunities, and perhaps including technical information about the services and the subjects covered by the centre. The newsletter should be published regularly, for example, monthly, and distributed as widely as possible. Consider whether you need to issue it in more than one language, depending on who the readers will be. Computer-assisted generation of the newsletter will make it easier to produce a version for the web, either using software capable of producing an image in Portable Document Format (pdf), which can be posted to the web, or software that can manipulate the same content to produce a printed and an electronic version (in the way that for example Microsoft Publisher can do). Some of the decisions you make will be dictated by your organization's policy on acceptable software.

A website is a great asset as it makes access available to the library or information centre 24 hours a day, seven days a week. It can be changed regularly and should always be up to date, designed so that viewers are encouraged to click on the front page for more information. We have added more references in the reading list to encourage you to create a website for your centre. You can provide a number of services electronically, including access to your catalogue and to digitized content via direct links from the catalogue.

Organizing seminars and training courses

Training can be aimed at people at all levels:

- managers and directors
- supervisors
- trade union members and representatives
- workers
- educators
- doctors and nurses
- journalists and editors
- members of the public.

There are various ways in which training can be given, for example, through:

- films and videos
- seminars, conferences, training courses
- courses on specific topics
- general awareness courses
- awareness of information services
- publications, both free and priced.

Once a library or information centre is established there will be increasing numbers of opportunities to organize seminars designed to demonstrate the range of areas in which it is active.

This may require the participation of specialists from all sections of the organization, in addition to contributions from information specialists. Organizing a seminar or conference requires the input of much time and effort, but the benefits in promoting the activities of the library or information centre are sufficient reward. The following pages describe some of the steps to be taken when organizing seminars and training courses.

Planning

Remember that it takes time to organize and adequately promote seminars and training courses. Consequently, you need to plan many months ahead. It is useful to plan a whole year's activities in advance and publish a diary of events so that potential audiences have advance notice of whatever seminars and training courses you are organizing.

The effects of seminars and training courses

In a normal teaching situation, students retain:

- **10%** of what they **read**
- **20%** of what they **hear**
- **30%** of what they **see**
- **50%** of what they **see** and **hear**
- **80%** of what they **say** as they **talk**
- **90%** of what they **say** as they **do**.

Learning is not a spectator sport!

Information awareness training courses for other specialists

Consider running awareness training courses for people whose specialism is not in information. In Chapter 9 we list some suggestions for outline programmes for various categories of potential information users. Each course has opportunities for question and answer sessions. The course contents could cover the following topics:

- management responsibilities, including legislation
- information and how to access it
- keeping up to date
- computerized systems
- fact finding and establishing a methodology for enquiries
- finding information in a wide variety of sources – journals, reports, legislation and so on.

These general headings are ones that we frequently come across, but each course can be tailored to the organization and to the people who are expected to attend.

How to organize seminars and training courses

There are a number of important steps in organizing a successful seminar or training course, including the following:

- Identify your audience.
- Decide on an appropriate subject.
- Decide the date of the event and its location.
- Organize speakers who can speak authoritatively on the subject.
- Organize handouts and publicity.
- Make sure all is well two weeks, one week and one day before the event.
- Run the event!
- Thank your participants and evaluate the event.

We look at this in more detail in Chapter 9. However, you may have someone who can help you internally with the organization, or consider whether it is worth hiring in a conference organizer for part or all of the work.

Training using videos

A well made video can successfully inform, educate and sometimes shock an audience into positive action. They are also quick, convenient and cost-effective to use. But even the best videos cannot do the job alone. They need to be presented in the right environment, to the right number of people and in the right way if the message is to be driven home properly. Don't just treat them like a sideshow. In Chapter 9 we tell you more about how to use videos.

Summary

This chapter looked at different types of promotional activity, and identified ways of targeting them appropriately. Hints and tips for each activity were given and ways of assessing their impact were discussed. We hope that this will show what an exciting range of opportunities are available to promote your library and information service.

9

Training, seminars and meetings

• •

In this chapter we look at:

- ideas for training
- target groups for training
- how to organize seminars and training courses
- training using videos or DVDs
- how to organize meetings
- planning ahead.

• •

There are a number of steps that need to be followed to ensure a successful seminar or training course. This chapter considers ways of identifying target groups in different sectors and of creating suitable training sessions.

Target groups

Target groups in public libraries are:

- children
- teenagers
- retired people
- business people
- sports groups
- trade unions
- associations
- information specialists from industry and commerce.

Target groups in academic libraries are:

* new undergraduates
* new lecturers
* postgraduate students
* distance learners.

Target groups in a special information sector such as health and safety are:

* the organization's staff
* trade union occupational health and safety representatives
* occupational health nurses
* information specialists from industry and commerce
* occupational health and safety practitioners.

You will quickly become aware of similar target groups for your own information centre.

How to organize seminars and training courses

Decide on the subject or topic of the training course

In the annual review of the provision of the information services a number of topics may be identified as possible topics for training sessions or open days. Examples are introducing a new piece of legislation, a new service or collection, or running an open day highlighting the various services on offer to encourage use of the information centre.

Decide on the date of the event and location

Book an available room where the meeting can take place. It is important to ensure that there is as little outside interference (for instance from telephones) as possible.

Seating should be arranged in either cinema or conference layout to suit the size of the audience, the style of the speakers and the physical limitations of the room. Some trainers prefer to use a U-shape layout for tables and chairs so that all the delegates can see each other.

Organize a video machine, film projector, overhead projector and any other equipment that may be needed by the speakers.

Organize speakers

Ensure that speakers know their subject well and can deliver a talk publicly to an audience. Brief them on what you require them to do, say and write, and if necessary meet them to discuss details. Keep in touch with the speakers, especially if the conference has been arranged some time ahead of the event.

Organize the publicity

Announce the seminar at least two months in advance by sending letters (direct mailshots) to individuals, organizations, libraries and information centres, trade unions and so on, stating the objectives, subjects to be covered, overall duration and price, and giving the names of the speakers. If there are to be demonstrations of online sources, CD-ROMs, films, videos, DVDs or other opportunities for access to information sources, mention it.

Ensure also that there are adequate supplies of information packs and other handouts. Successful seminars will 'self-promote' themselves; and there may be requests for the same or similar programmes to be mounted in other locations.

Send out adverts to all potential delegates with details of the course or seminar giving a description, details of the venue, date, time and speakers, strict instructions for payment of any fees to the organizer and a cut-off date for last application.

Once the publicity is on the way, the following steps need to be taken to ensure that the conference or training course is well planned.

Other steps to take if preparing for a conference or training course

Delegates

Organizers may wish to appoint a course director who will need details of where and when the course or conference is to be held, anyone else involved in the preparation, and list of delegates. The course or conference director may be responsible for all the detailed work involved in the meeting.

Organizers will need to start to make a list of names of delegates, and send letters or e-mails back to them accepting the fee and confirming a place on the course or at the conference.

Organization of handouts

Have extra copies of handouts and programmes run off and put them on a table at reception or hand them out when delegates are seated.

Have a list of names on sticky labels written out or have names printed off from the computer and inserted into plastic badge holders.

Training room(s)

Discuss with speakers or tutors in advance if they need:

- a personal computer, if using PowerPoint, Excel etc.
- a projector, either for overheads or to connect to a computer as required
- video recorder
- handouts, flipcharts and paper
- copies of any publications for reference purposes.

Also organize:

- chairs
- tables
- drinking water for speakers and chairperson, and for delegates.

Reception

Ensure that a list of names of delegates is sent to receptionists at the venue, in advance, and include speakers' names on the list.

Refreshments

Order refreshments as appropriate.

Speakers

Keep in touch with speakers and chairpersons if planning well ahead.

Two weeks before the event

Two weeks before the event check:

- that the room is still available
- that speakers are still available, what time they are arriving and if they need any overnight accommodation beforehand
- that any biographical notes about the speakers are still up to date
- what equipment speakers still need
- if equipment needed is still available
- if delegates' information pack is ready; it should include:
  — a programme for the day (with any changes to advertised programme)
  — a list of delegates
  — an evaluation form – this is a useful way of finding out how successful the event was from the delegates' point of view
  — a name badge or sticky label
  — any other publicity information.

One week before the event

Check everything is OK. Use above checklist.

On the day

Make sure that you:

- get to the venue at least one hour before start
- check equipment
- greet speakers on arrival
- ensure reception staff know what to do
- ensure each delegate has an information pack
- introduce conference programme or training course to delegates and give them details of domestic instructions
- introduce speakers to chairperson or course director.

Order of the day

If there is more than one speaker then introduce speakers to each other at registration. Remember to explain housekeeping information, such as:

- location of fire exit
- location of toilets
- location where refreshments are to be served
- security arrangements.

Outline of the day

The chairperson or course director will introduce the programme:

- stating the aims and objectives of the day
- giving details of each session and how the conference training course will be conducted
- explaining what the handouts in the delegate pack contain
- if appropriate, asking each delegate to introduce themselves
- asking delegates to fill in an evaluation form at the end of the course (this needs stating during the sessions as a reminder).

After the event

At the end of the event:

- check evaluation forms and note any comments for your next event
- write to thank speakers and chairpersons, send them any payment due and also, if possible, some feedback from delegates
- thank any others involved.

Training using videos or DVDs

A well made safety video or DVD can successfully inform, educate and sometimes shock an audience into positive action. Videos are also quick, convenient and cost-effective to use. But even the best safety videos cannot do the job alone. They need to be presented in the right environment, to the right number of people and in the right way if their message is to be driven home properly.

Group size

The ideal group size for a video presentation is 10–15 people. Smaller groups may be difficult to motivate. Larger groups may be difficult to control.

Room and group setting

Group seating positions are important to ensure a clear, unobstructed view of the visual aids (monitor, screen, flipchart, blackboard and so on) and the trainer at all times. The ideal room layout is a 'U' shape, which will facilitate group participation and group–trainer interaction.

Group participation

In general people like sharing their experiences and it is important to encourage group participation throughout. Following the video presentation, you may feel it beneficial to divide the audience into smaller discussion groups of three or four people. If possible try to ensure that these groups contain a mix of people – by gender, job type, experience. Different perspectives on the subject matter will often stimulate discussion and, again, encourage participation. Appoint a spokesperson for each group and change the spokesperson after each exercise.

Action plans

Try to ensure that the overall message put across by the video, the trainer and any support material you produce is consistent. Mixed messages can lead to confusion and a 'diluted' effect.

Remember what your training session is about and make sure that the room itself is a model of health and safety. For instance, there should be no exposed leads or trailing cables from audiovisual equipment. Cover them over or securely tape them to the floor.

Choose your own session plans

According to the size of audience or your own personal preference, you may wish to follow either of the following session plans:

Plan 1 – Interrupted video viewing

Introduction (5 mins) Introduce yourself and the objectives of the session.

Discussion (10 mins) Invite the group to summarize its perception of the subject matter and distribute any relevant support material.

Show the video Tell the group something about the video they are about to see. (It is essential that you are familiar with the video yourself. Watch it once or twice beforehand and, if necessary, make notes of relevant points and potential areas for discussion.)

Pause the video at the start of each relevant point. Ask and invite questions on these points, and, where appropriate, hand out any additional support material of particular relevance.

Final discussion (10 mins) Refer back to the session objectives and invite any final questions or comments. Thank the group for their participation.

Plan 2 – Uninterrupted video viewing

Introduction (5 mins) Introduce yourself and the session objectives.

Discussion (10 mins) Invite the group to summarize its perception of the subject matter; distribute any relevant support material.

Show the video Tell the group something about the video they are about to see and look out for any key points you may think relevant.

Run the whole video On completion break the group down into smaller, mixed groups and hand out any additional support material of particular relevance.

After the exercise, check to ensure that each trainee has fully understood each point and encourage discussion.

Final discussion Refer back to the session's objectives and invite any final questions or comments. Thank the group for their participation.

Organizing meetings

From time to time you are likely to want to organize meetings, for example to allow your library user committee to get together. How do you go about it? It's easy if you have a secretary or assistant (who will make all the arrangements), but what if you are a one-person operation?

What is a meeting?

Meetings consist of a few essential elements, and some optional ones. Your job is to get all of the necessary things to coincide, and if they do the result will be a successful meeting.

Essential items include the time and date, the place, the topic and the people. Who needs to be there? When and where will they meet? And what will they discuss? This sets the scene and makes the meeting possible. Optional elements include presentations, papers and external speakers. Doing without these will not stop the meeting going ahead or meeting its goal, but they can make it go more efficiently and effectively.

Who?: getting the meeting together

A meeting could consist of two people who agree to meet in a coffee bar at 10.30 on Monday morning to discuss induction for a new member of staff; but for a larger meeting arrangements need to be more formal.

Many meetings will need a chairperson, or someone to lead the discussion more or less formally. They will need someone else to keep a record (or 'minutes') of what is said, and to ensure that it is filed where everyone who needs to see it can find it. Bear in mind that in many organizations people now have a right to ask to see records of meetings under freedom of information legislation, so the minutes should be comprehensive and an accurate summary of the discussion and decisions. You can probably see that for anything but the smallest informal meeting you need separate people to chair and to be secretary.

Who else needs to be there? The answer to this will dictate the time and date of the meeting and maybe the place, too. If you work in an organization with an office network that includes a calendar or scheduler software, then things are easier, because you can find a slot in the timetables of the people you want to come to the meeting, and invite them to attend. Who is essential and whom can you do without? It can be very difficult to get half a dozen busy people together, so would it be acceptable if only four of them can make it? Who is the most important? Is it essential that one particular person is there because he or she wants to ask the meeting for a decision, or has to explain what has happened in connection with a particular topic? Decide the pecking order and, if you cannot get every person there, make sure that the key people can take part. Some of the others may change their schedule so that they can attend.

What?: the agenda

The topic or topics to be discussed are listed on an agenda. A good chairperson will keep the debate centred on items on the agenda, while allowing debate of relevant topics that come up during the meeting. The agenda needs to be sensible in terms of the time available (so that you do not have to discuss next year's budget in four and a half minutes flat) by taking account of the importance of the topics and the likely length of the debate. Don't worry if this is not obvious the first time you are asked to set up a meeting – err on the side of caution, as a short agenda is better than a hopelessly long one that has people looking at their watches long before the end of the meeting. On future occasions you will be able to combine topics, as you will have some idea of how long debate will last. If the same people are at each meeting they do not need to go back to the beginning of the debate on every occasion, but can build on their mutual understanding. Thus, if the staff budget is being discussed (as in the case study in Chapter 4) the first meeting might allow 30 minutes for a discussion of the requirements, but in later meetings it could be enough to allow ten minutes for questions on a written report of current spending.

Ask participants to provide written papers for topics they introduce, especially where there is a complex idea to get across. This is particularly helpful where someone is asking for a decision involving money or staff, where it helps to have the details explained on paper. Spend time in advance resolving any difficulties or disagreements, and in clarifying anything that people do not understand. Your meeting should not turn into a training course as people try to understand ideas that they could have got to grips with the evening before if they had seen the papers earlier. Make sure that you mark as confidential any papers involving finance and especially those that deal with identifiable people; destroy any copies that are not for the record when the meeting is over.

Where?: the venue

The other essential element for a good meeting is place. Meeting rooms are nice but not always available. If you have a large committee to house, consider the availability of a suitable room when you find out about the availability of people. Think creatively: boardrooms are not always occupied by the board, head teachers' studies are not always occupied by head teachers, and libraries are not always open. Ask whether any of these are possible locations.

If you cannot get a meeting room in your organization, you could hire one outside. Again, be creative: a local restaurant or pub may have a room that you could use, and some will let you have it for a couple of hours in return for a guaranteed spend on refreshments (which do not of course have to be alcoholic). Ask colleagues what they do if there are no spare rooms, and ask whether anyone in your networks of information professionals knows of suitable local facilities. You will probably have to pay for the room (and use real money rather than charging it to your internal budget) but you may find the meeting is more productive than being squeezed into a corner of the café in your organization's premises, so that there is a productivity gain that offsets the cost in the total balance sheet.

Don't let meetings run on too long. Have a finish time in mind, and aim to stick to it unless there are good reasons. If you are in the chair, you may want to set a rough timetable for yourself so that all the important business is dealt with efficiently. Try to bring discussion to a conclusion in good time so that everyone has a say and a decision is made if necessary. It is far more difficult to do this if people have had to leave to catch trains, or if everyone is looking at their watch every five minutes. Sometimes there are good reasons why a meeting has to go on past the proposed finish time, but the fact that some people like the sound of their own voice is not one of those reasons!

Optional extras: papers, presentations and external speakers

As we saw when we discussed the agenda above, having papers for a meeting helps people prepare in advance and makes the meeting more productive. It will not always be possible to distribute papers in advance, however, so allow people time to read any documents tabled on the day. It may be helpful to ask the author of a paper to make a presentation in addition to talking the meeting through the paper. You may need to provide a computer and projector, as many people find it easier to use presentation software as a means of focusing people's attention and of ordering their ideas.

Sometimes you will want to invite an external speaker to a meeting, such as a representative of a company offering software or a library supply service that you are interested in. Let your speaker know how long he or she will be able to talk, whether there will be questions, and whether they are invited to the rest of the meeting (which could either inhibit discussion on other items, or be useful to help discussion of those same items, so you need to judge carefully). Remember to allocate someone to escort the visitor to and from the meeting, as the chairperson and secretary are likely to be too busy to do this.

Larger meetings, open days and conferences

What about larger meetings, like library open days? A lot of the same principles apply to these meetings, too. You need the time, place and people, although the topic may be a bit more difficult to pin down if you are not running a formal conference. Nevertheless it's worth trying to define what you are doing, so that you can attract the visitors you want by telling them what the event is about and what they will gain from being there.

It will probably be more complicated to get the people you need together for an open day or a conference with presentations. If you do not have many terminals available, or you are arranging for your suppliers to bring their own equipment, then you will have to agree a timetable for the presentations. A conference will usually have one computer, attached to a digital projector, onto which all the presentations are loaded in advance. This is much simpler than having people bring along their own laptops and trying to get those to connect to the projector. You should ask speakers to send you a file on disc or by e-mail some days or weeks before the meeting – this will not only ensure that you can read the file, but it will make sure the work is finished in time! Try to avoid having speakers or presenters turning up on the day, so that you need a technician to load discs and virus check files in real time (which can often be three minutes before the speaker is due to start . . .). Ask for files in standard format (which is almost always Microsoft PowerPoint) and suggest that they should not be over-large, maybe a target size not above 1Mb.

Be prepared for people to ask whether they can take copies of interesting presentations on memory sticks; decide first of all how you will ensure that these are virus free if you are going to allow it. A good alternative method is to put the presentations onto your intranet. This allows other people in your community to read the files, and print them out if they wish, so that people who could not be at your event can see what went on.

This approach also increases the traffic to your information centre's website and spreads the message about your services.

Publishing a report of your meeting

For major meetings you can consider publishing the proceedings or at least a summary report. This again will raise your profile in the organization, and nowadays can be done using print on paper or by using an electronic format such as Portable Document Format (PDF), which is the proprietary file format created by Adobe Acrobat and some other software. It has the advantage of being widely used, and that the software to read it is available free from the internet or on the cover discs of many computer magazines. If your organization has a computer network it is very likely that PDF is a standard format and you already have software to read it; maybe there is software to create it, too, either as a standalone program or embedded as an option for saving files in your word processor software.

If you go for print on paper you will have to do your calculations carefully to see whether it is viable to publish. Ask for quotations if this is appropriate (you may have to use your organization's print shop and pay their prices) and decide whether you can afford not to recoup the costs. Be honest about the number of copies to be printed and distributed. The set-up costs mean that printing a small number of copies of a publication costs more per copy than for a long run. On the other hand there is no point in printing 2000 copies of a pamphlet to get cheaper costs per copy if you only expect to send out 200 of them. Is it worth printing just 200 or will you have to stick to electronic publishing?

Electronic publishing has the advantage that the print costs are carried by the reader, who also has the choice between colour and monochrome printing. If you prepare colour documents (which of course look far more professional than black and white, and generally have greater impact) the print costs are higher than for black and white. In electronic format there is no difference in costs for colour, and you can use monochrome illustrations for impact rather than because they are cheaper. You may have access to electronic publishing software (such as Microsoft Publisher, Adobe PageMaker or Quark), which will give you advanced features, but for many purposes recent word processing software has surprising flexibility and will allow you to create professional-looking results mixing text and illustrations in accurately laid out pages. As we advise in a number of cases, this is an occasion when you should decide what you want to achieve and seek advice from a specialist when you reach the limits of your own knowledge. Don't spend days creating a document that your print shop can't reproduce!

Plan ahead

For an open day or conference style of meeting, it is important to plan well ahead. You will be incredibly lucky to get all the people you need at one month's notice – you may need to book them at least three months in advance. Especially if your participants are expected to prepare a presentation, aim to give as much notice as possible. Have one or two extra people on standby and tell them you will call on them if someone drops out. Ask them to prepare their talk anyway, and add it to your website. Give disappointed speakers first refusal for your next open day.

Organizing and running meetings can be hard work but can also be a lot of fun. For anything more than a routine meeting, it may be best to get a small committee together to share the work of contacting people, obtaining rooms, ordering refreshments, chairing, minuting, and otherwise organizing and recording the meeting.

Summary

In this chapter we have looked at two important activities for many libraries and information centres: user training and organizing meetings. We have seen that both are straightforward and simple if you bear in mind what you are trying to achieve.

We have looked at ideas for training, and identified different kinds of users and potential users who could be encouraged to use the information services. Various ideas and step-by-step guidelines have been suggested on how to organize successful seminars or training courses.

We have offered hints from our own experience, which we believe will give you confidence in making a mark for your service, and may have others seeking your advice on how to carry out these activities with the same success as you enjoy!

Glossary

In this section are terms and definitions that will assist you in setting up your library and information service (LIS) from scratch – although they are not necessarily all used in the text of this book. As your LIS develops you will find it useful to have definitions of services and activities to include in your brochures, business plans or service level agreements (SLAs).

Abstracting: making and recording on the LIS database a summary of the information in a document that has been catalogued and/or indexed there.

Additional library and information services: services in addition to those listed in your service level agreement or brochure about basic services. (In the SLA these are typically enumerated and described in an annexe to the agreement.)

Advisory services: advice on the indexing of publications, or on the organization and classification of collections, or on other information resources held within the LIS.

Alerts *see* **Current awareness service**

Balance sheet: a list of income and expenses by date or by category of expenditure.

Best value: 'The duty of Best Value is one that local authorities will owe to local people, both as taxpayers and the customers of local authority services. Performance plans should support the process of local accountability to the electorate. Achieving Best Value is not just about economy and efficiency, but also about effectiveness and the quality of local services the setting of targets and performance against these should therefore underpin the new regime.' Department of the Environment Transport and the Regions, press release *New Duty of Best Value for Local Authority Services*, 15 September 1999.

Binding: a job carried out usually by a professional bookbinder – either a book that needs its cover replaced or a number of issues of a journal that will be bound together into one volume.

Book jobber, also called a 'purchasing agent': a company that orders books for libraries and information services.

Bookplate: a label with the name of the library that can be glued onto a blank page at the front of a book. It can also have space for the name of the person or place that donated the book. This is distinct from a date label, used to record to date an item for loan is due for return.

Browser box: a place to put interesting or new materials that you want users to see.

Budget: the sum of money provided by the organization or community for the operation of the LIS, probably expressed as an annual amount of money. It may be subdivided, e.g. into bookfund, staff salaries budget, periodicals fund, electronic databases fund, and so on: and the amounts fixed may include an element for value added tax on certain purchases or for costs associated with salaries such as earnings-related national insurance contributions (ERNICs).

Card catalogue: a cabinet with drawers for holding book cards, which usually come in one of a range of standard sizes.

Catalogue: a complete list of the books in the LIS. Some common types of catalogues are author catalogues, subject catalogues (classified catalogues) and title catalogues. The library management systems currently on the market offer computerized catalogues or databases that offer these and other views of the records they contain.

Cataloguing: the creation of bibliographic records according to stated and agreed standards, and their incorporation into the LIS database.

CD-ROM (compact disc – read only memory): a small disc made of metal and plastic used for electronically storing databases, text, images, sounds and software. Identical in size and similar in appearance to an audio CD, these are being superseded by DVD-ROMs (see below), which have far larger storage capacity.

Change control: a means of agreeing and recording changes to contracts or SLAs using procedures specified in the agreement. It is likely to include a statement showing whose consent is required to any changes, how these are to be recorded, and whether there is any time limit to them (i.e. whether they run for the remainder of the agreement and become part of it for renewal purposes, or whether they take place for a fixed length of time). It is also likely to record the location of a master copy of the contract which is agreed by all parties to be the definitive version.

Circulation: the process of lending books to users (but see also below).

Circulation of periodicals (circulation management): the distribution of consecutive issues of periodicals to their users throughout the organization, passed on in sequence using a circulation list based on customers' requests to receive copies on circulation. You may choose not to make certain periodicals available on circulation or for use outside the LIS. When you provide electronic journals, the circulation of either the title, table of content and/or full text is of course simultaneous to all readers.

Collection development policy: a written description of what materials the library will stock (e.g. by important subjects, languages, reading levels, age, etc.) and how donations will be used. It may also describe materials the library does not want (e.g. damaged, outdated, sexist, racist, etc.).

Classification: the process of sorting non-fiction books into different subject categories. Commonly used systems include the Dewey Decimal Classification (DDC), the Universal Decimal Classification (a more complex system often used for technical collections) and the Library of Congress Classification (frequently used in academic libraries).

Compulsory competitive tendering (CCT): a form of testing the efficiency and cost-effectiveness of a current in-house service(s), much used in UK local government. Compare with **Market testing**.

Committee: a management committee overseeing the LIS, which in many organizations will include a majority of members who do not have professional information qualifications and who will therefore require careful guidance by the LIS staff.

Consensus: a policy or decision made when all the members of a group reach an agreement on an issue.

Copyright advice: Advice to company departments on aspects of copying from published sources. In many UK organizations this will include administration of photocopying licences to the LIS from the Copyright Licensing Agency, the Newspaper Licensing Agency, the Ordnance Survey and other collecting societies, and advice to departments on licensed copying.

Current awareness service (or Alerts): sometimes known as Selective Current Awareness News Service, or SCANS, this is a service that provides a regular list of recently acquired LIS materials likely to be of interest to customers (e.g. based on an individual's interests, or reflecting the interests of divisions in a given organization). It can include new book titles, journal articles and reports.

Dewey Decimal Classification (DDC): a standard system for arranging non-fiction books by subject.

Distance learning: courses taken by post or using the internet.

Disposal of publications: the disposal of materials no longer required by customers or sections. Your collection policy document should include a section setting out your approach to disposals and donations.

Document supply: the supply of photocopies or extracts from documents in LIS stock. The service should be regulated by the provisions of the law of copyright, plus any concessions available under the copyright licences you hold.

Alternatively, document supply can mean the supply of extracts from documents held in remote databases by commercial and other suppliers, regulated by agreements in force concerning the copyright in those documents.

Donations: items given to the LIS by its users. See under Disposal of publications above.

DVD-ROM (digital versatile disc – read only memory): a newer form of storage on disc, identical in format to the discs used for domestic viewers, but capable of storing up to 4.7 gigabytes of data. See also CD-ROM.

e-delivery: electronic delivery of documents, journals and other information, for example via the internet, websites, CD-ROM, DVD-ROM, or other electronic means.

e-mail: electronic messages sent from one computer to another using the internet or an intranet. They can be delivered to a range of devices, including not only computers but mobile telephones and personal digital assistants (PDAs) such as the Blackberry.

Enquiry and reference services: answering enquiries on all subjects of corporate interest, based on a collection of publications held as reference material and/or for lending at the main LIS and branches, and using external sources to support these collections.

Externalization: provision of all aspects of a current service through a company or trust established for the purpose. Compare this with **Outsourcing**.

Fiction: materials about imaginary characters, places or events (e.g. stories).

Indexing: the creation or enhancement of bibliographic records with terms from an indexing language (i.e. a list of subject terms) in order to allow their later retrieval for current awareness or in response to enquiries.

Information retrieval: the retrieval and presentation of selected records taken from remote computer-held databases, or from databases (on CD-ROM, DVD-ROM or hard disc) held in the LIS. Searches can be carried out by LIS staff, using information provided by the customer, although some specialist customers may be given direct access to the databases after suitable training.

Information resources: all of the ways that people obtain information, including books, newspapers, radio, television and direct communication with other people.

Interest: money paid by the bank to people holding accounts with a positive balance. People who owe money to the bank have to pay interest to the bank. The amount of the interest is usually a percentage of the balance in the account. Note that many suppliers will impose interest on invoices that remain unpaid after a stated period of time such as 30 days.

Interlibrary loans: loans of material borrowed from other LIS arranged through the XYZ Co. LIS for its customers.

Internet: an international network of computers that can be used to send and receive **e-mail** (see above), access information on the **world wide web** (see below) and exchange information and data in other ways.

Internet service provider: a company that provides its customers with e-mail or world wide web access. Customers connect their computer with the company's computer (called a server) by dial-up (over a standard telephone line) or by broadband connection. Your computer must be connected to a server in order to check your e-mail or browse the web.

Inventory: all of the materials in the LIS. 'Taking an inventory' means checking to see if any materials are missing from the library.

Junior Colour Code: a version of the **Dewey Decimal Classification** (see above) used by school libraries.

Line item budget: a list of all the library's expenses and income by the type of expense (e.g. new books) or income (e.g. a grant, or even the proceeds of a raffle).

Loan of LIS material: a service of lending documents from the LIS stock to customers in XYZ Co. for notified durations of time.

Market testing: UK government initiative used to test effectiveness, efficiency and costing of service providers against external providers. Compare with **Compulsory competitive tendering**.

Networking: the process of researching and contacting people and organizations that can help the LIS.

Non-fiction: materials that contain facts and information.

Nongovernmental organization (NGO): private groups working for the public good. They are also called charities, non-profits, aid organizations, relief organizations and other names depending on the type of work they do and the location.

Operating manual (or operations manual): a manual describing the rules and procedures used in the LIS. It should include information about how the stock is organized and circulated, how records are kept, the duties of the librarian or information officer, and any other helpful information about running the LIS. It must be kept up to date, and can be used as a basis for a training manual for new staff or staff undertaking new duties.

Outsourcing: contracting whole or part of the activities to an outside organization or individual. Compare this with **externalization**.

Periodical: any item such as a newspaper, magazine or annual report that is published regularly (periodically). Most periodicals have a volume number, issue number and/or date on the front cover.

Publisher: a company, NGO, government agency or other organization that produces and distributes books, periodicals, teaching aids, electronic media and/or other resources.

Purchase of publications for retention: The purchase and provision of documents specified by LIS customers for purposes that make the provision of a loan copy or copies inappropriate. Many LIS make this service subject to any restrictions on supply brought about by the state of their budget or other conditions at their discretion.

Quorum: the number of committee members needed to make a vote official. It is usually at least half the members plus one.

Reference books: books that contain general information on many subjects, such as dictionaries, almanacs, yearbooks and encyclopedias.

Selective dissemination of information (SDI): a service providing current information from the LIS, or from external databases, to selected customers or groups of customers in the company, by matching the indexing terms of newly published materials with the search profiles of customers.

Shelf list: a list of all the materials in the library according to their location on the shelves.

Subject category: a topic used for sorting books. The topics can either be selected by the librarian or taken from the classification scheme used.

Subject code: a short way of writing a subject category, such as HE for Health.

Subject index: a list of all the subject categories and codes used in the library.

Suggestion box: a facility for library users to deposit written comments about the functioning of the library, typically in the form of a letter box or other container with a slot to ensure confidentiality between the LIS and the client.

Term of office: the length of time that committee members serve as president, vice-president, treasurer, secretary or committee member.

URL (uniform resource locator): the address of an electronic document or 'page' on the **world wide web** (see below). In order to use a URL, you must type it into software for browsing the web while your computer is connected to the internet.

Value Added Tax (VAT) (see also **Budget**): tax paid on some materials purchased by the LIS. At the time of going to press, in the UK this includes electronic information services, elements of some subscriptions, telephone services, photocopying and some printing, but LIS managers should check the current position and take appropriate advice. In some other EU countries printed publications are subject to VAT, and prices will include an element for tax.

Vertical file: a box or cabinet with folders for storing pamphlets, clipping and other small items on different topics.

World wide web: part of the internet that displays text and multimedia. The web allows access to a wide range of information and entertainment resources such as street maps, encyclopedias, music from around the world, newspapers, radio and television from different countries, and a wide range of educational materials in many languages. To use the web, you need a computer, web browser software and an account with an internet service provider. To connect to the internet you can use a dial-up modem, or for higher speed access either broadband or ISDN access is available in many areas of a growing list of countries.

References and further reading

We have listed the references to text quoted in the various chapters and also added other references for those with further curiosity.

Facet Publishing (formerly Library Association Publishing) books are available from Bookpoint Ltd, Mail Order Dept, 39 Milton Park, Abingdon, Oxon OX14 4TD, UK. Tel: +44 (0)1235 400400. Fax: +44 (0)1235 832068/861038. E-mail: orders@bookpoint.co.uk

Further information: www.facetpublishing.co.uk; www.sheilapantry.com/books
E-mail: sp@sheilapantry. com
All websites checked 2 August 2005.

Chapter 1 Back to basics

Baird, N. (1994) *Setting Up and Running a School Library*, London, VSO Books/Heinemann, ISBN 0435923048.

Boddy, D., Boonstra, A. and Kennedy, G. (2005) *Managing Information Systems: an organisational perspective,* 2nd edn, Harlow, Financial Times/Prentice Hall, ISBN 0273686356.

Brassell, D. (2005) Building a Library from Scratch: teaching Pre K-8, January,
www.findarticles.com/p/articles/mi_qa3666/is_200501/ai_n9466526

Brophy, P. et al. (eds) (2000) *Libraries Without Walls 3: the delivery of library services to distant users. Proceedings of an international conference organized by CERLIM, 10–14 September 1999,* London, Library Association Publishing, ISBN 1856043770.

Covello, J. and Hazelgren, B. J. (1998) *Your First Business Plan: a simple question and answer format design to help you write your own plan*, 3rd edn, Naperville IL, Sourcebooks Trade, ISBN 1570712190.

Gates, K. (2001) Librarians are Finding Endless Opportunities, *Managing Information*, **8** (2), 58.

Goulding, A., Bromham, B., Hannabuss, S. and Cramer, D. *Likely to Succeed: attitudes and aptitudes for an effective information profession in the 21st century*, Library and Information Commission research report 8, www.mla.gov.uk/information/legacy/lic_pubs/researchreports/

Griffiths, P. (2001) All that Glitters: the role of the information professional in handling rogue information on the internet, *Online Information 2001: proceedings*, Oxford, Learned Information, 17–23.

LaGuardia, C. and Mitchell, B. A. (1998) *Finding Common Grounds: creating the library of the future without diminishing the library of the past*, New York, Neal-Schuman Publishers, Inc., ISBN 1555702902.

LaGuardia, C. (1998) *Recreating the Academic Library: breaking virtual ground*, New York, Neal-Schuman Publishers, Inc., ISBN 1555702937.

Lankes, R. D., Collins, J. W. and Kasowitz, A. S. (eds) (2000) *Digital Reference Service in the new Millennium: planning, management and evaluation*, New York, Neal-Schuman Publishers, Inc., ISBN 1555703844, The New Library Series Number 6.
The book is easy and exciting to read, and contains a useful list of bibliographic references and websites to resources on digital reference in a variety of contexts. This resource list will be updated regularly online at www.vrd.org/pubinfo/proceedings99_bib.shtml

Leicestershire Careers and Guidance Services Ltd (2001) *Setting up a Careers Library Handbook,* Leicester, Leicestershire Careers and Guidance Services Ltd.

Porter, K. (2003) *Setting Up a New Library and Information Service*, Oxford, Chandos, ISBN 1843340534 (paperback), ISBN 1843340542 (hardback).

Taylor, J. (2001) *How to Manage Information Technology Projects: a systems approach to managing IT software, hardware, and integration tasks,* London, McGraw-Hill Publishing Company, ISBN 0814405878.

Tegart, S. (2001) *Setting up a Library from Scratch,* Special Libraries Association, Western Canada, www.sla.org/chapter/cwcn/wwest/v5n1/tegart.htm

Tuominen, K. Monologue or Dialogue in the Web Environment: the role of networked library and information services in the future, *66th IFLA Council and General Conference, Jerusalem, 13–18 August 2000*, www.ifla.org/IV/ifla66/papers/004-131e.htm

Wendell, L. (1998) *Libraries for All! How to start and run a basic library,* United Nations Educational, Scientific and Cultural Organization,. www.eldis.org/static/DOC6656.htm

The electronic resources acquired by libraries and information centres include: computer software, databases, news feeds, daily financial information sources; see www.arl.org/scomm/licensing/licbooklet.html

Chapter 2 The first steps

Allen, B. *InfoMapper Instructor's Guide,* for use with InfoMapper software (but sold separately), Washington DC, Information Management Press, Inc., ISBN 0960640835.

Basch, R. (1995) *Electronic Information Delivery – ensuring quality and value,* Aldershot, Gower, ISBN 0566075679.

Batt, C. (1998) *Information Technology in Public Libraries*, 6th edn, Library Association Publishing, ISBN 1856042537.

Bird, J. (1997) *The Reuters Guide to Good Information Strategy*, London, Reuters, ISBN 1901249050.

Burk, C. F. Jr. and Horton, F. W. Jr. (1991) *InfoMap: the complete guide to discovering corporate information resources*, Prentice-Hall. Now available from Information Management Press, Inc., PO Box 19166, Washington DC 20036, USA, ISBN 013464476.

Central Computer and Telecommunication Agency (1990) *Managing Information as a Resource*, London, CCTA, TSO, ISBN 011330529X. A practical guide showing policy guidelines and how to conduct an information audit. Though oriented towards government departments, this slim book is a handy guide; it is available from the bookshop at The Stationery Office.

Davenport, T. and Prusak, L. (1998) *Working Knowledge: how organizations manage what they know*, Boston, Harvard Business School Press.

Deegan, M. and Tanner, S. (2001) *Digital Futures: strategies for the information age*, London, Library Association Publishing, ISBN 1856044114.

Gorman, G. E. (2001) *Information Services in an Electronic Environment: International Yearbook of Library and Information Management 2001–2002,* London, Library Association Publishing, ISBN 1856044033.

Griffiths, P. (2004) Performing an Information Audit: identifying gaps and areas in need of development, *Content Management Focus,* **3** (4), 13–17. Reprinted in *Compliance and Beyond: information management compliance 2004/5,* supplement to *ei magazine,* **1** (5), 10–13.

Henczel, S. (2001) *The Information Audit: a practical guide,* Information Management Series, Munich, K. Saur, ISBN 359824367777.

Hildebrand, C. (1995) Information Mapping: guiding principles, *CIO: the Magazine for Information Executives,* **8** (18), 60–4.

Horton, F. W. Jr. (1983) *The Information Management Workbook: IRM made simple,* revised and updated 3rd edn, loose-leaf three-ring binder, Washington DC, Information Management Press, Inc., ISBN 0960640800.

Horton, F. W. Jr. (1988, 1989) Mapping Corporate Information Resources, three-part series of articles in the *International Journal of Information Management,* **8,** 249–54; 1989, **9,** 19–24 and 91–5.

Horton, F. W. Jr. (1991) Infomapping, *The Electronic Library,* **9** (1), 17–19.

Hyams, E. (2001) Nursing the Evidence: the Royal College of Nursing information strategy, *Library Association Record,* **103** (12), 747–9.

Jantz, Ronald C. (2001) Technological Discontinuities in the Library: digital projects that illustrate new opportunities for the librarian and the library, *IFLA Journal,* **27,** 2, 74–7.

Jones, R. and Burwell, B. (2004) Information Audits: building a critical process, *Searcher: the magazine for database professionals,* **12** (1), (January), 50–6.

Journal of Knowledge Management, IFS International Ltd, Wolseley Business Park, Kempston, Bedford MK42 7PW, UK.

Lankes, R.D., Collins, J. W. III and Kasowitz, A. S. (2000) *Digital Reference Service in the New Millennium: planning, management and evaluation,* New Library Series Number 6, New York, Neal-Schuman Publishers, Inc., ISBN 1555703844.

Lannon, R. *InfoMapper Project Manager's Guide,* for use with InfoMapper software (but sold separately), Information Management Press, Inc., PO Box 19166, Washington DC 20036, USA, ISBN 0960640851.

MacLachlan, L. (1996) *Making Project Management Work for You,* London,

Library Association Publishing, ISBN 1856042030.

McCracken, C. (2001) Illumination not Enumeration: information audits are not a counting exercise but a platform from which to develop a total KM strategy, *Dialog Magazine,* 10–13.

Ming, D. C. (2000) Access to Digital Information: some breakthroughs and obstacles, *Journal of Librarianship and Information Science,* **32** (1), 26–32.

Nielsen, J. (1998, 1999) Reputation Managers are Happening, *Alertbox,* 5 September 1999, www.useit.com/alertbox/990905.html; The Reputation Manager, *Alertbox,* 8 February 1998, www.useit.com/alertbox/980208.html

Orna, E. (1999) *Practical Information Policies,* London, Gower Press, 2nd edn.

First published in 1990 this second edition provides a strategic management perspective on information management and relates it well to knowledge management. It is a good practical guide with excellent guidance for those developing and implementing information management. This edition has 14 new case studies from the UK, Australia and Singapore.

Pan, R. and Higgins, R. (2001) Digitisation Projects at Durham University Library – an overview, *Program,* **35** (4), 355–68.

Pantry, S. (ed.) (1999) *Building Community Networks: strategies and experiences,* London, Library Association Publishing, ISBN 1856043371.

Pantry, S. and Griffiths, P. (1998) *Becoming a Successful Intrapreneur,* London, Library Association Publishing, ISBN 1856042928.

Pantry, S. and Griffiths, P. (2000) *Developing a Successful Service Plan,* Successful LIS Professional Series, London, Library Association Publishing, ISBN 1856043924.

Pantry, S. and Griffiths, P. (2001) *The Complete Guide to Preparing and Implementing Service Level Agreements,* 2nd edn, London, Library Association Publishing, ISBN 1856044106.

Pantry, S. and Griffiths, P. (2002) *Creating a Successful E-information Service,* London, Facet Publishing, ISBN 1856044424; Lanham MD, Scarecrow Press, 2003, ISBN 0810847787.

Pantry, S. and Griffiths, P. (2003) *Your Essential Guide to Career Success,* 2nd edn, London, Facet Publishing, ISBN 1856044912.

Pantry, S. and Griffiths, P. (2004) *Managing Outsourcing in Library and Information Services,* London, Facet Publishing, ISBN 1856045439.

Pedley, P. (2002) Resources Revealed: tracking down newspapers and journals on the web, *Managing Information,* **9** (1), 48–9.
This article suggests a number of websites that can help users to locate the sites of newspapers and journals, or at least the details of who publishes them

Rees-Jones, L. and Kidd, T. (eds) (2000) *The Serials Management Handbook: a practical guide to print and electronic serials management,* London, Library Association Publishing, ISBN 185604355X.

Reuters Business Information (1996) *Dying for Information? An investigation into the effects of information overload in the UK and worldwide,* London, Reuters Business Information, www.cni.org/regconfs/1997/ukoln-content/repor~13.html

Reuters; Ronin Research Services (1997) *Glued to the Screen: an investigation into information addiction worldwide,* London, Reuters, ISBN 0901249068, www.healthyplace.com/Communities/Addictions/netaddiction/bio/reuters.html

Smith, K. (1999) Delivering Reference Services to Users Outside the Library, paper presented to: *1999 and Beyond: partnerships and paradigms,* Sydney, September, http://www.csu.edu.au/special/raiss99/papers/ksmith.html

Special Libraries Association *Towards Electronic Journals* (Virtual SLA), www.sla.org/content/Shop/towelecjnl.cfm

Tanner, S. (2001) Librarians in the Digital Age – planning digitisation projects, *Program,* **35** (4), 327–37.

TFPL Ltd (1999) *Skills for Knowledge Management: a briefing paper,* based on research undertaken by TFPL on behalf of the Library and Information Commission, LIC. Executive summary and full text at www.mla.gov.uk/information/legacy/lic_pubs/executivesummaries/kmskills.htm

Software

InfoMapper software package, IBM Compatible Standalone PC Version (Release 1.2 Mod. 1) user manual, ISBN 0960640843, LAN also available, as well as French, Spanish and German language IBM compatible PC versions. Information Management Press, Inc., PO Box 19166, Washington DC 20036, USA.

Information Mapping, Inc., 411 Waverley Oaks Road, Waltham MA 02452-8470, USA, Tel: +1 781 906-6400 or (800) INFOMAP (463-6627), www.infomap.com, E-mail: inquiry@infomap.com (also European and South African associates).

Chapter 3 Establishing the library and information service

Think health and safety and take notice of the guidance and advice published by various authoritative organizations around the world, e.g. UK Health and Safety Executive (HSE), US National Institute for Occupational Safety and Health (NIOSH) and the European Agency for Safety and Health at Work. See the reading lists of publications on the following websites www.hse.gov.uk, www.cdc.gov/niosh, http://osha.eu.int

Akeroyd, J. (2001) The Management of Change in Electronic Libraries, *IFLA Journal*, **27** (2), 70–3.

Borgman, C. (1986) Why are Online Catalogs Hard to Use?, *Journal of ASIS*, **37** (6), 387–400.

Borgman, C. (1996) Why are Online Catalogs Still Hard to Use?, *Journal of ASIS*, **47** (7), 493–503, www.sims.berkeley.edu/courses/is202/f01/borgman.pdf

Griffiths, J.-M. (1999) Why the Web is not a Library, *FID Review*, **1** (1), 13–20.

Jacquesson, A. (2000) De la Difficulté à Utiliser les Bibliothèques Numériques, *Bulletin d'information [Association des Bibliothécaires de France]*, **188**, 3e trimestre, www.abf.asso.fr/IMG/pdf/n188_2.pdf

Jantz, R. (2001) E-books and New Library Service Models: an analysis of the impact of e-book technology on academic libraries, *Information Technology and Libraries*, **20** (2).

Jatkevicius, J. et al. (2000) Free Legal Resource Aggregators on the Web, *Econtent*, October/November, **23** (5), 27–34.

Law, D. (1997) Parlour Games: the real nature of the Internet, *Serials*, **10** (2).

Muet, F. (1999) Services et Revues Électroniques dans l'Enseignement Supérieur: synthèse de quelques enquêtes récentes sur les usages, *Bulletin des bibliothèques de France*, **44** (5), 18–23.

Pinfield, S. (2001) Managing Electronic Library Services: current issues in UK higher education institutions, *Ariadne*, **29**, www.ariadne.ac.uk/issue29/pinfield/

Quigley, B. (2000) Physics Databases and the Los Alamos e-Print Archive, *Econtent*, **23** (5), 22–6.

Rusbridge, C. (1998) Towards the Hybrid Library, *D-Lib Magazine*, (July/August), www.d-lib.org/dlib/july98/07rusbridge.html

Rusbridge, C. and Royan, B. (2000) Towards the Hybrid Library: developments in UK higher education, *66th IFLA Council and General Conference, Jerusalem, 13–18 August 2000*, www.ifla.org/IV/ifla66/papers/001-142e.htm

Smith, K. (1999) Delivering Reference Services to Users Outside the Library. In *1999 and Beyond: partnerships and paradigms, RAISS Conference, Sydney, 6-8 September 1999*, Sydney, NSW, Reference and Information Services Section, Australian Library and Information Association.

Special Libraries Association (2003) Special Committee on Competencies for Special Librarians. *Competencies for Special Librarians of the 21st Century*, rev. edn, June 2003, prepared for the Special Libraries Association Board of Directors by the Special Committee on Competencies for Special Librarians: Eileen Abels, Rebecca Jones, John Latham, Dee Magnoni, Joanne Gard Marshall, SLA, Alexandria, VA 22314-3501, USA, www.sla.org/content/learn/comp2003/index.cfm

Yeates, R. (2003) Reputation Management for Libraries; overcoming reluctance to collaborate. Paper presented at *Interlend 2003: breaking barriers*, New Hall, Cambridge, July 2003, www.cilip.org.uk/groups/fil/c2003k.html

Websites

e-brary (www.ebrary.com)

Lucent Technology Foundation (www.lucent.com). A press release about the Partnership in Global Learning is at www.lucent.com/press/0300/000309.coa.html

Partnership in Global Learning (http://grove.ufl.edu/~pgl)

Chapter 4 Staffing

Australian Library and Information Association (1997) NT Libraries Serve Diverse People in Remote Locations, Kingston NSW, ALIA. Press release, 4 May 1997, for Australian Library Week, www.alia.org.au/media.room/1997.05.04c.html

Brown, D. J. (2001) The Impact of Disintermediation and the New Economy on STM Electronic Information Systems, *Serials,* **14** (1), 47–55.

Chu, H. (2000) Promises and Challenges of Electronic Journals: academic libraries surveyed, *Learned Publishing,* **33** (3), 169–75.

Clegg, B. (2001) *The Professional's Guide to Mining the Internet, Information Gathering and Research on the Net,* 2nd edn, London, Kogan Page, ISBN 0749435557.

Dorr, J. and Akeroyd, R. (2001) New Mexico Tribal Libraries, *Computers in Libraries,* **21** (9), 36–42. A grant from the Bill and Melinda Gates Foundation has funded the Native American Access to Technology Program.

Gordon, A. C., Gordon, M. T. and Moore, E. J. (2001) *Library Patrons Heavily Use Public Access Computers and Other Library Services, and Want More: a report to the Bill and Melinda Gates Foundation US Library Program on a Survey of Library Patrons in Five States.* Public access to computing project, Evans School of Public Affairs, University of Washington, www.gatesfoundation.org/nr/downloads/libraries/eval_docs/pdf/Patron_501.pdf

Goulding, A. et al. *Likely to Succeed: attitudes and aptitudes for an effective information profession in the 21st century,* Library and Information Commission research report 8, London, Library and Information Commission, www.mla.gov.uk/information/legacy/lic_pubs/researchreports/#rr8

ISO 23950:1998 Information and Documentation – Information Retrieval (Z39.50) – Application Service Definition and Protocol Specification, International Standards Organization.

King, D. W. and Tenopir, C. (2004) Scholarly Journal and Digital Database Pricing: threat or opportunity? In MacKie-Mason, J. and Lougee, W. J. (eds) *Bits and Bucks: economics and usage of digital collections,* Cambridge MA, MIT Press. Also available at http://web.utk.edu/~tenopir/eprints/database_pricing.pdf

Lankes, D. et al. (eds) (2000) *Digital Reference Service in the New Millennium: planning, management and evaluation,* New Library Series Number 6, New York, Neal-Schuman Publishers, Inc., ISBN 1555703844. The book is easy and exciting to read, and contains a useful list of bibliographic references and websites to resources on the topic of digital reference in a variety of contexts. This resource list is updated regularly online at www.vrd.org/pubinfo/proceedings99_bib.shtml

O'Flynn, S. (2001) Giving Them What They Want, *Information World Review,* (September), 28.

Owen, T. B. (2003) *Success at the Enquiry Desk: successful enquiry answering – every time,* 4th edn, London, Facet Publishing, ISBN 1856044777.

Pantry, S. and Griffiths, P. (1998) *Becoming a Successful Intrapreneur,* London, Library Association Publishing, ISBN 1856042928.

Pantry, S. and Griffiths, P. (2001) *The Complete Guide to Preparing and Implementing Service Level Agreements,* 2nd edn, London, Library Association Publishing, ISBN 1856044106.

Pantry, S. and Griffiths, P. (2003) *Your Essential Guide to Career Success,* 2nd edn, London, Facet Publishing, ISBN 1856044912.

Peters, T. J. and Waterman, R. H. (1982) *In Search of Excellence,* New York, Harper and Row, ISBN 0060150424.

Pinchot, G. (n.d.) www.pinchot.com/MainPages/BooksArticles/InnovationIntrapreuring/TenCommandments.html

Reuters Business Information (1996) *Dying for Information? An investigation into the effects of information overload in the UK and worldwide,* London, Reuters Business Information, www.cni.org/regconfs/1997/ukoln-content/repor~13.html

Reuters; Ronin Research Services (1997) *Glued to the Screen: an investigation into information addiction worldwide,* London, Reuters, ISBN 0901249068, www.healthyplace.com/Communities/Addictions/netaddiction/bio/reuters.html

Skills for Knowledge Management: a briefing paper by TFPL Ltd based on research undertaken by TFPL on behalf of the Library and Information Commission, LIC, June 1999, www.mla.gov.uk/information/legacy/lic_pubs/executivesummaries/kmskills.htm

Tenopir, C. and King, D. W. (2001) Lessons for the Future of Journals,

Nature, (18 October) , **413** (6857), 672–4.

Argues that science journals provide major benefits and will continue to thrive.

Tenopir, C. et al. (2001) Scientists' Use of Journals: differences (and similarities) between print and electronic. In *National Online 2001: proceedings*, USA, Information Today Inc., 469–82.

Chapter 5 Information networks

Association of Independent Libraries (n.d.),
  www.independentlibraries.co.uk/

Australian National Library (n.d.), www.nla.gov.au/copiesdirect/

Batt, C. (1995) Networking for the World, *Library Association Record*, Year in Review Supplement, **97** (12), 13.

Briefly shows the various public library initiatives in networking – Golden Valley Project, ITPoint, Croydon Libraries Internet Project, Stumpers Network, Project Earl and so on.

British Library (n.d.), www.bl.uk/services/document.dsc.html

Circle of State Librarians (1993) *Change in Libraries and Information Services: managing change or changing managers?*, London, HMSO, ISBN 0118875426.

Various papers given at the annual Circle of State Librarians conference showing how professional information staff must be able to adapt, manage change and change ideas of others. One paper discusses networking by talking to customers to ensure they are aware of the many and varied services on offer. Papers are: Managing Change and Changing Managers, by Maurice B. Line; Managing the Changing Environment: working with people, by Stuart A. Morgan; Planning for Success: an outline, by Sylvia P. Webb; and The Future of Co-operation Including Networking, by Jean Plaister.

Circle of State Librarians (1994) *Networking and Libraries: technological innovation and the transformation of information services*, London, HMSO, ISBN 0118875477.

Various papers showing how technologies are employed in the various government departments' and agencies' information services.

Circle of State Librarians (1995) *Who Needs Libraries? Challenges for the 90s*, London, HMSO, ISBN 011887548.

This includes a number of important papers on the changing roles of libraries particularly within government information service; includes market testing surviving the new world and freedom of information.

Foreman, L. (ed.) (1993) *Change in Libraries and Information Services*, London, HMSO, ISBN 0118875426.

Information Society Forum (1996) *Networks for People and their Communities. Making the most of the information society in the European Union.* First annual report to the European Commission from the Information Society Forum, June 1996. *Cordis Focus* (1996), supplement 10.
Gives the background and overview of the way the technologies will change the way people will work and live.

Krechowiecka, I. (1998) *Net that Job: using the WWW to develop your career and find work*, London, Kogan, ISBN 0749425741.

Lester, R. (ed.) (2005, 2006, 2007) *The New Walford: guide to reference resources*, London, Facet Publishing, Vol. 1, Science, Technology and Medicine, 2005; Vol. 2, The Social Sciences, 2006; Vol. 3, Arts, Humanities and General Reference, 2007.

LIBRI (1991) **41** (4) contains the following papers: Networking and You, by Sheila Pantry; Networking, by Jean Plaister; The New Age of Reconnaissance: networks for the faint hearted, by Robin Yeates; Networking on a University Campus and its Effect on Library Services, by Emma Cusworth; Co-operation and Networking Between French Libraries, by Christine Deschamps; The Impact of Networking on International Interlibrary Loans and Documents Supply by Graham P. Cornish; Projects ION (OSI pilot/demonstration project between Library Networks in Europe for Interlending Services), by Jean Plaister.

Open Directory (n.d.) http://dmoz.org/Reference/Libraries/

Pantry, S. (ed.) (1999) *Building Community Information Networks: strategies and experiences*, London, Facet Publishing, ISBN 185604337 1.

SINTO (n.d.) http://extra.shu.ac.uk/sinto/info_intro.htm

Truffield, J. (1995) Personal Networking, *Managing Information*, **2** (10), 26–7.
Shows the importance of effective networking.

Ward, S. (1999) Information Professionals for the Next Millennium, *Journal of Information Science*, **25** (4), 239–47.

While not exactly on networking this presidential address to the Institute of Information Scientists Annual General Meeting and Members' Day on 17 September 1998 gives an overview of the skills needed for the new millennium information worker.

Discussion groups

The Washington Library Research Consortium (WRLC) maintains a list of mainly US discussion lists of interest to the LIS profession. See www.wrlc.org/gsdl/cgi-bin/library?p=about&c=liblists It includes the useful 'Liblicense-l' list at www.library.yale.edu/~llicense/

In the UK, JISCMail hosts 25 lists of interest in this area, many of them open to all readers; see www.jiscmail.ac.uk/category/P2.html. Of these, LIS-e-journals and LIS-e-books are probably of most interest to many readers of this book.

Major francophone resources are listed at www.francopholistes.com/espaces/metiers/documentalistes.shtml They include the discussion lists of the main French and Belgian professional bodies (ADBS and ADB-VDB) and two widely used lists, biblio-fr http://listes.cru.fr/wws/arc/biblio-fr and Resonet which publishes a fairly regular e-bulletin at http://actu.ladoc.net/

German resources and several English and French language projects are listed at www.bib-info.de/komm/knt_neu/fundgrub/bib_dig.htm

A list of digital library resources is maintained by Google at http://directory.google.com/Top/Reference/Libraries/Digital/

Chapter 6 Services to be provided by the library and information service

Albany University on the Developing National Library Network Statistics and Performance Measures project, http://www.albany.edu/~imlsstat/

Ball, D. and Pye, J. (2000) Library Purchasing Consortia: the UK periodicals supply market, *Learned Publishing*, **13** (1).

Ball, D. and Wright, S. (2000) Procuring Electronic Information: new business models, *Library Consortium Management: an international journal*, **2** (7), 145–58.

Bertot, J. C., McClure, C. R. and Ryan, J. (1999) Developing National Public Library Statistics: performance measures for the networked environment: analysis of State Library data elements for networked information resources and services, www.albany.edu/~imlsstat/state.analysis.pdf

Bevan, S. (2001) Replacing Print with E-journals – Can it be Done? A case study, *Serials*, **14** (1), 17–24.

Boyle, F. (2001) Veni Vidi Non Vici: e-journals management at the University of Liverpool, *Serials*, **14** (1), 25–32.

Brennan, P., Hersey, K. and Harper, G., *Licensing Electronic Resources: strategic and practical considerations for signing electronic information delivery agreements*, Washington DC, US Association of Research Libraries, www.arl.org/scomm/licensing/licbooklet.html

Brophy, P. (2001) Electronic Library Performance Indicators: the EQUINOX project, *Serials*, **14** (1), 5–9.

Brophy, P. and Wynne, P. M. Management Information Systems and Performance Measurement for the Electronic Library: eLib Supporting Study (MIEL2) MIEL (Management Information in Electronic Libraries) final report, www.ukoln.ac.uk/dlis/models/studies/mis/mis.rtf

Byrd, S. et al. (2001) Cost/benefit Analysis for Digital Library Projects: the Virginia Historical Inventory Project, *The Bottom Line: managing library finances*, **14** (2), 65–75.

Copyright and Related Rights Regulations 2003 (SI 2003 No. 2498); available at www.opsi.gov.uk/si/si2003/20032498.htm

Cornford, J. (2001) A Costing Model for a Hybrid Library Shell, *Library Management*, **22** (1/2), 37–8.

Duncan, M. (1997) The Electronic Library at Work, *Managing Information*, **4** (5), 31–4.

The EQUINOX project, funded by the Telematics for Libraries programme funded by the European Commission, has developed a set of proposed performance indicators for electronic libraries. See http://equinox.dcu.ie/reports/pilist.html

ESYS Consulting (2001) Summative Evaluation of Phase 3 of the E-Lib Initiative: final report, Guildford, ESYS, Section 5.2, 50.

Falk, H. (1999) Projecting the Library onto the Web, *Electronic Library*, **17** (6), 395–9.

Fialkoff, F. (2001) Rising Costs and NetLibrary, *Library Journal*, (15 December).

GALILEO Planet, winter 2002, 1, www.usg.edu/galileo/planet/planet_winter_draft3_final.pdf

Griffiths, P. (2004) *Managing your Internet and Intranet Services: the information and library professional's guide to strategy*, 2nd edn, London, Facet Publishing, ISBN 1856044831.

Gyeszly, S. D. (2001) Electronic or Paper Journals? Budgetary development and user satisfaction questions, *Collection Building*, **20** (1), 5–10.

ICOLC, the International Coalition of Library Consortia, has developed guidelines for service measurement: International Coalition of Library Consortia (2001) *Guidelines for Statistical Measures of Usage of Web-based Information Resources*, rev edn, www.library.yale.edu/consortia/2001webstats.htm

Landesman, M. (2001) The Cost of Reference, *Library Journal*, reference supplement, 15 November.

Law, C. (2000) PANDORA – Towards a National Collection of Selected Australian Online Publications. In *IFLA, 66th IFLA Council and General Conference*, Jerusalem, 13–18 August 2000, www.ifla.org/IV/ifla66/papers/174-157e.htm

Marunet e-services supply arm, www.maruzen.co.jp/home-eng/marunet.html

McCracken, C. (2001) Illumination Not Emuneration: information audits are not a counting exercise but a platform from which to develop a total KM strategy, *Dialog Magazine*, (December), 10–13.

Owen, T. B. (2003) *Success at the Enquiry Desk: successful enquiry answering - every time*, 4th edn, London, Facet Publishing, ISBN 1856044777.

Pantry, S. and Griffiths, P. (1998) *Becoming a Successful Intrapreneur: a practical guide to creating an innovative information service,* London, Library Association Publishing, ISBN 1856042928.

Pantry, S. and Griffiths, P. (2001) *The Complete Guide to Preparing and Implementing Service Level Agreements*, 2nd edn, London, Library Association Publishing, ISBN 1856044106.

Pantry, S. and Griffiths, P. (2002) The Internal Information Audit: conducting the audit and implementing the results, *Business Information Review,* **19** (1).

Pantry, S. and Griffiths, P. (2004) *Managing Outsourcing in Library and Information Services*, London, Facet Publishing, ISBN 1856045439.

Pascoe, R. and Black, H. M. (2001) Virtual Libraries – Long Overdue: the Digital Agenda Act and Australian libraries, *Australian Library Journal*, **50** (2), (May), www.alia.org.au/alj/50.2/full.text/virtual.libraries.html

Pinfield, S. (2001) *Beyond E-lib: lessons from Phase 3 of the Electronic Libraries programme*, [s.l.], [s.n], www.ukoln.ac.uk/services/elib/papers/other/pinfield-elib/elibreport.pdf

Rusbridge, C. and Royan, B. (2000) *Towards the Hybrid Library: developments in UK higher education. In IFLA, 66th IFLA Council and General Conference, Jerusalem, 13–18 August 2000,* www.ifla.org/IV/ifla66/papers/001-142e.htm

Sloan, B. (n.d.) Library Consortia Documents Online, Urbana Champaign IL, University of Illinois, www.lis.uiuc.edu/~b-sloan/consort.htm
The Graduate School of Library and Information Science provides a collection of useful documents for the establishment and management of such groups.

Spiteri, A. (2001) Unpublished presentation on Elsevier services during session 'Les Enjeux Économiques et Culturels de la Numérisation', 18th IDT conference, Palais des Congrès, Paris, 29–31 May.

Vickery, J. (2000) Reorganisation in the British Library to Acquire Electronic Resources. In IFLA, *66th IFLA Council and General Conference, Jerusalem, 13–18 August 2000,* www.ifla.org/IV/ifla66/papers/116-180e.htm

Woodward, H. (2001) Usage Statistics. Presentation to the *e-ICOLC conference*, Espoo Meripuisto, Finland, November 2001, http://www.lib.helsinki.fi/finelib/digilib/eicolc/Woodward.ppt

Subscription agents

See Appendix 5.

Managing suppliers

Ball, D. and Pye, J. (1999) Library Purchasing Consortia in the UK: activity and practice, *Library and Information Briefings,* **88**, 1–15.

Building Relationships with Suppliers, themed issue, *TQM Magazine*, **5** (5).

CPI Ltd (1998) Changing Relationships: new dimensions in library supply. Proceedings of a seminar held in December 1998, Bruton, CPI Ltd, ISBN 1898869499.

Eden, R. (1998) Bookfund Tendering, Assessment and Evaluation – the Librarian's Viewpoint, *Taking Stock*, 7–11.

Gambles, B. (2000) Procurement: new skills for best value?, *Library and Information Appointments,* (11 August), **3** (17), App 373–4.

Greenhalgh, N. (1993) Managing *Supplier Relationships*, London, HMSO.

Hardwood, P. and Prior, A.(1998) The Role and Service of Subscription Agents, *Library and Information Briefings*, **81**, 2–12.

Inger, S. (2001) The Importance of Aggregators, *Learned Publishing*, October, **14** (4), 287–90.

Lancaster, N. (1998) Bookfund Tendering, Assessment and Evaluation – the Supplier's Viewpoint, *Taking Stock*, 1–6.

Naylor, C. (2000) When the Supplier Selects, *Bookseller*, (18 February), 28–9.

Naylor, C. (2000) Liverpool Scores with Supplier Selection, *Bookseller*, (2 June), 28–9.

Sidebottom, D. (1998) Tendering for Library Services and Supplies, *Serials*, **11** (3), 224–5.

Wootton, D. (1999) Managing your Service Suppliers, *Managing Information*, **6** (4), 41–3.

Managing e-suppliers

Bates, M. E. (1998) How to Implement Electronic Subscriptions: replacing the routing list hassle, *Online, (*May), 80–6.

Lister Cheese, A. (2000) Electronic Information Resources from Swets Blackwell. In *e-OSHE World: seeing the future*, conference, Dublin, Ireland, Friday 23 June 2000, www.kosha.net/jsp/servlet/control.userbbs.down.DownUserBbs?x= 444&FILE=SwetsBlackwell.ppt e-mail: Alistercheese@uk.swetsblackwell.com

Percy, R. Library Services Managing Successful Outsourcing in the
Digital Age. In *Digital Library Technology 97: transforming library services
for the digital age – meeting user needs for electronic information delivery*,
207–21. IES Conference, Chatswood, NSW, Australia.

Chapter 7 Support for the library and information service

Deconinck, C. and Gauchet, P. (1998) Gravelines Grand-Fort Philippe
(Nord): deux approches différentes de l'exploitation d'intranet,
Bulletin d'Informations, Association des Bibliothécaires Français
(3e–4e trimestre 1998), 184–5 .
ISO 23950:1998 Information and Documentation – Information
Retrieval (239.50) – Application Service Definition and Protocol
Specification; ISO 9004-2 *Quality Management for Services and ISO 9001
Total Quality Management*, International Standards Organization.
Continually evolving – see latest editions.
Leigh, A. and Maynard, M. (1997) *Perfect Communications: all you need to
get it right first time*, New York, Random House, ISBN 0099410060.

Professional library and information associations

American Library Association
www.ala.org
Australian Library and Information Association
www.alia.org.au/alw/index.html
British and Irish Association of Law Librarians
www.biall.org.uk
British Association for Information and Library Education and Research
(BAILER)
www.bailer.ac.uk/
Chartered Institute of Library and Information Professionals
www.cilip.org.uk
European Association for Health Information and Libraries (EAHIL)
www.eahil.net/
European Bureau of Library, Information and Documentation
Associations (EBLIDA)

www.eblida.org/
European Information Association
www.eia.org.uk
International Federation of Library associations and Institutions (IFLA)
www.ifla.org
Library Association of Ireland
www.libraryassociation.ie/
Medical Libraries Association (USA)
www.mla.org
Others can be found via University of Exeter:
www.library.ex.ac.uk/internet/wwwlibs.html#liborgs

Chapter 8 Promoting the library and information service

Marketing

Coote, H. and Batchelor, B. (1998) *How to Market your Library Service Effectively*, 2nd edn, London, Aslib, ISBN 0851423965.

De Sáez, E. E. (2002) *Marketing Concepts for Libraries and Information Services*, 2nd edn, London, Facet Publishing, ISBN 0851574262.

Hart, K. (1998) *Marketing your Information Services*, London, Library Association Publishing, ISBN 1856041824.

Hamilton, F. (1990) *Infopromotion*, Aldershot, Gower, ISBN 0566055775.

Leigh, A. and Maynard, M. (1993) *Perfect Communications: all you need to get it right first time*, New York, Random House, ISBN 0099410060.

Library Association (1997) *Marketing Library and Information Services: LA training package*, London, Library Association Publishing, ISBN 185604274X.

TFPL Ltd. (1999) *Skills for Knowledge Management: a briefing paper*, based on research undertaken by TFPL on behalf of the Library and Information Commission, London, LIC. Executive summary and link to full text at
www.mla.gov.uk/information/legacy/lic_pubs/executivesummaries/kmskills.html

Keeping one step ahead of your competitors

Covey, S. R. (2005) *The Seven Habits of Highly Effective People: restoring the character ethic*, London, Simon and Schuster, ISBN 084858398.

Pantry, S. and Griffiths, P. (1998) *Becoming a Successful Intrapreneur: a practical guide to creating an innovative information service*, London, Library Association Publishing, ISBN 1856042928.

Pantry, S. and Griffiths, P. (2001) *The Complete Guide to Preparing and Implementing Service Level Agreements*, 2nd edn, London, Library Association Publishing, ISBN 1856044106.

Chapter 9 Training, seminars and meetings

Leigh, A. and Maynard, M. (1993) *Perfect Communications: all you need to get it right first time*, New York, Random House, ISBN 0099410060.

Library Association, *Marketing Library and Information Services: LA training package*, London, Library Association Publishing, ISBN 185604274X.

Pantry, S. and Griffiths, P. (1998) *Becoming a Successful Intrapreneur: a practical guide to creating an innovative information service*, London, Library Association Publishing, ISBN 1856042928.

Glossary

The following references describe various projects that will be of interest and give more definitions of services and initiatives.

Brophy, P. (2000) *The Library in the Twenty-first Century: new services for the information age*, London, Library Association Publishing. ISBN 1856043754. (See in particular Chapter 5, 'What is a Library?: digital and hybrid libraries'.)

Hampson, A. (2001) Practical Experiences of Digitization in the BUILDER Hybrid Library Project, *Program*, **35** (3), 263–75.

Higher Education Resources On-Demand, www.heron.ingenta.com/

Law, C. (2000) PANDORA – towards a national collection of selected Australian online publications. *66th IFLA Council and General Conference, Jerusalem, 13–18 August 2000*, www.ifla/org/IV/ifla66/papers/174-157e.htm

NHS Information Authority (2000) *National Electronic Library for Health*, [s.l.], London, NHS Information Authority.

NHS Information Authority (2000) *NELH-PC: primary care National electronic Library for Health*, London, NeLH-PC Project Team.

NOVEL (2001) New York Online Virtual Electronic Library: libraries expanding information access for New Yorkers in the 21st century, New York, NOVEL Planning Team, ftp://unix2.nysed.gov/pub/state.lib.pubs/novel/finalpln.pdf [accessed 12 July 2005].

Pinfield, S. and Dempsey, L. (2001) The Distributed National Electronic Resource (DNER) and the Hybrid Library, *Ariadne*, **26**, (January), www.ariadne.ac.uk/issue26/dner/intro.html [accessed 12 July 2005].

Appendices

Appendix 1
Copyright declaration form

The following wording could be used on your information service's copyright declaration form.

Name of Information Service
Address
Date

Please supply me with a copy of an article in a periodical, or part of a published work, as described overleaf, required by me for the purposes of **non-commercial** research or private study.
  I declare that:

- I have not previously been supplied with a copy of the same material by you or any other librarian.
- I will not use the copy except for research **for a non-commercial purpose** or private study and will not supply a copy of it to any other person.
- To the best of my knowledge no other person with whom I work or study has made or intends to make, at or about the same time as this request, a request for substantially the same material for substantially the same purpose.
- If this item is delivered by an electronic method (including fax), I will retain only a single paper copy and destroy any electronic copies after printing.

- I understand that if the declaration is false in a material particular the copy supplied to me by you will be an infringing copy and that I shall be liable for infringement of copyright as if I had made the copy myself.

Name

Address

Date

Signature

Appendix 2
List of basic reference books and periodicals

Quick reference

To start a quick reference section within an information centre, in addition to stock relevant to the organization, the following types of reference books would be useful and it is recommended that the centre invests in:

General

- A dictionary of the language of your country
- An English language dictionary – e.g. Oxford or Collins.
  Oxford dictionary of English, Oxford, Oxford University Press, 2003. ISBN 0198613474.
  Collins English dictionary : complete and unabridged, London, Harper Collins, 2004, ISBN 0007197527
- a technical dictionary
- an atlas of the world, for example *The Times comprehensive atlas of the world*, London, HarperCollins, 2003, ISBN 0007157207.
- maps of towns, cities, regions, and the country.

Basic online look up is available from a number of Cambridge University Press dictionaries at http://dictionary.cambridge.org and from the Compact Oxford English Dictionary at www.askoxford.com. The site www.dictionarylink.com provides links to these and other resources, while www.dictionary.net links to Webster's and eight other sources of technical and specialist English dictionaries.

Small extracts from the UK Ordnance Survey are available through www.ordnancesurvey.co.uk/oswebsite/getamap/. Ordnance Survey mapping is used by www.streetmap.co.uk which has a variety of scales and some aerial photography. The site www.multimap.co.uk is an alternative source of UK mapping down to street-by-street detail. Similar mapping is available for many European countries, for example through the French website www.iti.fr which includes town plans of many European locations, not just France.

Almanacs and reference works

A & C Black, 37 Soho Square, London W1D 3QZ
www.acblack.com
Produces a range of general reference such as:

- *Black's Medical Dictionary*
- *Whitaker's Almanac* – wide subject coverage
- *Who's Who* – biographies.

Content from these and other resources is available online, some of it free of charge and some at a cost. The major sources are KnowUK, www.knowuk.co.uk and X-Refer, www.xreferplus.com.

Directories

CBD Research Ltd produces a wealth of directories. Look at the website **www.cbdresearch.com** for its current directories, which include:

- *Centres, Bureaux and Research Institutes*
  4th edn. 2000, £125, ISBN 0900246855
- *Councils, Committees & Boards including Government Agencies and Authorities*
  13th edn. 2004, £163, ISBN 0900246952
- *Current British Directories*
  14th edn. 2003, £165, ISBN 0900246936

- *Current European Directories*
  3rd edn. 1994, £140, ISBN 0900246642
- *Directory of British Associations and Associations in Ireland*
  17th edn. 2004, £195, ISBN 0900246960
- *Directory of British Associations on CD-ROM*
  5th edn. 2003, £250+VAT
- *Directory of European Industrial and Trade Associations*
  6th edn. 1997, £195, ISBN 090024674X
- *Directory of European Professional and Learned Societies*
  6th edn. 2004, £147.50, ISBN 090024691X
- *Pan-European Associations*
  3rd edn. 1996, £94, ISBN 0900246731

Guides to sources of company information

- *American Companies Guide*
  1st edn. 1997, £78, ISBN 0900246685
- *Asian and Australasian Companies Guide*
  1st edn. 1993, £87, ISBN 0900246618
- *European Companies Guide*
  4th edn. 1992, £80, ISBN 0900246448

CBD can be contacted at:

CBD Research Ltd
Chancery House
15 Wickham Road
Beckenham
Kent BR3 5JS
UK
Tel: 0871 222 3440
Tel: +44 (0) 20 8650 7745
Fax: +44 (0) 20 8650 0768
www.cbdresearch.com

Other common information sources held by information centres cover
travel information and maps; and information about people, such as may

be found in telephone directories. Several useful resources are also now readily available on the world wide web, some of them based on the printed resources that were, until recently, commonly kept in the reference sections of many libraries.

UK rail travel, the OAG Rail Guide (formerly the ABC guide) has been published for over 150 years (www.oag.com); or the national rail timetables can be obtained from the internet (ojp.nationalrail.co.uk/planmyjourney/).

UK telephone information can be obtained from www.bt.com , or from 192 (www.192.com) which enables people to access facilities such as the electoral registers. 192.com has fees for the more advanced features, but basic information already freely available in the public domain is not charged for; while bt.com places a daily limit on the number of searches that can be performed. Information about UK postal addresses is available from the Royal Mail website (www.royalmail.com) but again there are limits to the number of searches that can be performed. Registration on some of these sites gives larger daily quotas of searches that may save a small information centre from needing a subscription.

Also check out *Success at the Enquiry Desk: successful enquiry answering – every time*, by Tim Buckley Owen, 4th edn, Facet Publishing, ISBN 1856043827. This contains a guide to key reference sources.

Handbooks

Keep any locally or nationally produced health and safety handbooks, and any relevant subject handbooks.

Statistics

The UK Office for National Statistics is the major source for UK official statistics. The online virtual bookshelf has a very extensive range of information on all subjects:

- agriculture, fishing and forestry
- commerce, energy and industry
- compendia and reference
- crime and justice
- economy

- education and training
- health and care
- labour market
- natural and built environment
- population and migration
- public sector and other
- social and welfare
- transport, travel and tourism.

See **www.statistics.gov.uk/onlineproducts/default.asp**.

Write to other well known publishers, and ask to be put onto their mailing list to receive catalogues, e-mail updates and further information about their publications.

Appendix 3
Example of a press release

A press release could be sent to various recipients, depending on the nature of the information in it. It could go to:

- departments and sections internally
- other information and library services, locally, nationally and internationally
- to the media – radio, TV and newspaper or journal – locally and nationally.

Press releases are reasonably cheap to produce on the computer using Microsoft templates. Refer to Chapter 8, 'Promoting the library and information service' for further details. An example is given below:

Sheila Pantry Associates Ltd

Press Release No. 3   Date

Setting up a Library from Scratch . . . Back to Basics
Setting up a Library from Scratch is a guide to help those who need to set up a library or information service in their organization, irrespective of subject background or type of organization. It will help those who have qualifications but no experience in setting up such a centre, and will guide those who have had no training at all.

The authors, Sheila Pantry OBE and Peter Griffiths, have had many years' experience setting up information services in different subject backgrounds for a wide range of organizations in the UK and other countries.

This book will 'hold your hand' as you tackle the many steps to take as you create a successful information service – irrespective of size. Remember small is beautiful! The book covers:

- what information is needed, how quickly and in what quantities (information audit approach)
- how to meet the information needs of special users
- premises and furniture
- equipment and internet access
- technical requirements
- staffing
- managing budgets and finance
- managing people – staff and management
- networking and locating sources of information
- promotion of the information centre.

Extensive reading lists are provided for each chapter of the book, which also has a full list of appendices of sample documents, from newsletters and press releases to lists of basic reference books and periodicals.

Facet Publishing September 2005 192pp paperback 1-85604-558-7 £29.95
Available from Bookpoint Ltd, Mail Order Dept, 39 Milton Park, Abingdon, Oxon OX14 4TD, UK
Tel: +44 (0)1235 400400. Fax: +44 (0) 1235 832068/861038.
E-mail: orders@bookpoint.co.uk
Further information – e-mail: sp@sheilapantry.com

Appendix 4
Example of an information centre's brochure

A brochure could be reasonably cheap to produce on a computer, in A4 folded format, perhaps on coloured paper, divided into two or three pages.

An example of a three-page brochure is shown in Figure A4.1.

Opening times	Logo of organization	Photo of centre or logo
Map of location	Staff contacts Names:	**XYX Information Services** Address:
	Tel:	Tel:
		Fax:
	e-mail:	e-mail:
		Website:
Page 5	Page 6	Page 1

Figure A4.1 Example of an information centre brochure

Details of parent organization	XYZ information service provides:	XYZ information service
Details of information service	• an enquiry service	is equipped with a computerized information retrieval system capable of accessing, searching and retrieving worldwide information via the internet, intranet and CD-ROMs.
	• reference services	
	• photocopies	
Aims and objectives:	• regular updates on specific topics	
	• lists of references	
• to collect, process, produce and disseminate information to users within the organization	• journals	
	• a regular newsletter	
	• literature searches.	
		Information can be sent to your desktop computer.
• to design appropriate training courses.		
Page 2	Page 3	Page 4

Figure A4.1 *Continued*

Appendix 5
Suppliers, subscription agents and searching the internet

Check out CILIP's buyers' guide, **www.cilip.org.uk/buyersguide/**.
Systems and furniture suppliers are listed below.

Systems suppliers

ADLIB Information Systems Ltd
Berkeley House
Hunts Rise
South Marston Park
Swindon SN3 4TG
Tel: +44 (0) 845 658 9484
Fax: +44 (0) 845 658 9487
e-mail: sales@ukadlibsoft.com
www.adlibsoft.com

Fretwell-Downing Informatics
Brincliffe House
861 Ecclesall Road
Sheffield S11 7AE
Tel: +44 (0) 114 281 6040
Fax: +44 (0) 114 281 6041
e-mail: enquiries@fdisolutions.com
www.fdisolutions.com

SIRSIDynix Ltd
Unicorn House
Station Close
Potters Bar
Herts EN6 3JW
Tel: +44 (0) 1707 858000
Fax: +44 (0) 1707 858111
e-mail: sales@sirsi.co.uk
www.sirsidynix.com, UK offices www.sirsi.co.uk and (for Great Britain)
www.dynix.com/home.asp?engl

Soutron Ltd
The Lodge
Highgate House
Burley Hill
Derby DE22 2ET
Tel: +44 (0) 870 950 6080
Fax: +44 (0) 870 950 6081
e-mail: info@soutron.com
www.soutron.com

Talis
Knights Court
Solihull Parkway
Birmingham Business Park
Birmingham B37 7YB
Tel: +44 (0) 870 400 5000
Fax: +44 (0) 870 400 5001
E-mail: sales@talis.com
www.talis.com

Tribal Technology
St Mary's Court
55 St Mary's Road
Sheffield S2 4AN
Tel: +44 (0) 114 281 6100
Fax: +44 (0) 114 281 6021
e-mail: tribaltechnology.co.uk
www.tribaltechnology.co.uk

Furniture suppliers

Demco Interiors
Phoenix House
54 Denington Road
Wellingborough
Northants NN8 2QH
Tel: +44 (0) 1933 445300
Fax: +44 (0) 1933 442764
e-mail: enquiries@demcointeriors.co.uk
www.demcointeriors.co.uk

F. G. Library Products Ltd
6 Charter Gate
Clayfield Close
Moulton Park
Northampton NN3 6QF
Tel: +44 (0) 1604 671571
Fax: +44 (0) 1604 671701
e-mail: library@fggroup.co.uk
www.fglibrary.co.uk

Finnmade Furniture Solutions Ltd
Lynton House
6 Newlands Lane
Hitchin
Herts SG4 9AY
Tel: +44 (0) 1462 452001
Fax: +44 (0) 1462 452002
e-mail: info@finnmade.co.uk
www.finnmade.co.uk

Gresswell Direct
Grange House
Geddings Road
Hoddesdon
Herts EN11 0NT
Tel: +44 (0) 1992 454511

Freefax: 0800 616634
e-mail: enquiries@gresswell.co.uk
www.gresswell.com

Librex Educational Ltd
Colwick Road
Nottingham NG2 4BG
Tel: +44 (0) 115 950 4664
Fax: +44 (0) 115 958 6683
e-mail: sales@librex.co.uk
www.librex.co.uk

Remploy Library Solutions
Remploy Furniture
Baglan Energy Park
Port Talbot SA12 7AX
Tel: +44 (0) 870 850 6100
Fax: +44 (0) 870 850 6200
e-mail: furniture@remploy.co.uk
www.remployfurniture.co.uk

Serota Library Furniture
92 Hilliard Road
Northwood
Middlesex HA6 1SW
Tel: +44 (0) 1923 840697
e-mail: info@serota.co.uk
www.serota.co.uk

Subscription agents and intermediaries

The Association of Subscription Agents and Intermediaries (ASA) is the professional body for subscription agents. The **ASA Members Directory** provides details of each member and gives information (where it has been supplied by the member) on their services, the range of periodicals they supply, the subjects covered, to whom and in which countries, and the promotional services offered to publishers.

See **www.subscription-agents.org/** for a full listing of members worldwide. Some of the main subscription agents are listed below.

Ebsco

4th Floor, Kingmaker House
Station Road
New Barnet
Herts EN5 1NZ
Tel: +44 (0) 20 8447 4200
Fax: +44 (0) 20 8440 2205
e-mail: mailuk@ebsco.com
www.ebsco.com

Infocandy

Golden Cross House
8 Duncannon Street
London WC2N 4JF
Tel: +44 0800 085 7893
Fax: +44 (0) 20 7408 9473
e-mail:info@infocandy.com
www.infocandy.com

Ingenta

23–38 Hythe Bridge Street
Oxford OX1 2ET
Tel: +44 (0) 1865 799000
Fax: +44 (0) 1865 799111
e-mail: libraryinfo@ingenta.com
www.ingentaconnect.com

Maruzen Company Ltd

Ireland House
150–151 New Bond Street
London W1Y 8AQ
Tel: +44 (0) 20 7409 0288
Fax: +44 (0) 20 7629 3515
e-mail: london-office@maruzen.co.jp
www.maruzen.co.jp

Swets Information Services
Swan House
Wyndyke Furlong
Abingdon
Oxon OX14 1UQ
Tel: +44 (0) 1235 857500
Fax: +44 (0) 1235 857501
e-mail: info@uk.swets.com
http://informationservices.swets.com/uk

Searching the internet

The internet is a combination of thousands of computers and connections – radio, cable and satellite – which link them together. It is one of the world's fast growing communication developments, and has created many information resources that can be of value to everyone who needs to stay ahead in their own specialism.

Making the best use of these resources takes time. Just as no one book will give all the answers to a question, you may not find the information that you need from looking at just one website such as the one for OSH WORLD (**www.oshworld.com**).

In this section you will find a variety of other sources that you can make use of in order to answer your queries, and some tips for searching, to save you time and costs. It covers the following topics:

- connecting to the internet
- internet terminology
- how to search effectively
- Usenet newsgroups
- mailing lists
- search engines
- Boolean logic operators.

Connecting to the internet

Connecting to the internet need not be expensive. Because of the flexibility of the internet, the hardware specifications for a computer to be use to connect to the internet are minimal. New computers are now generally 'internet ready'. The choice of connection and set-up will be determined by individual preferences. The local computer store or internet service provider you choose will help you decide.

Once you have selected a computer with appropriate networking hardware how you make your connection will depend on your organization's policies. Many organizations limit the use of the internet, but if your organization allows connection your computer section will be able to help you get started.

If you are connecting from home, then many services such as CompuServe or Pipex will provide the software and connection instructions.

Internet terminology

Many people find the jargon and acronyms surrounding the internet confusing. Here is some guidance.

The **world wide web** (**WWW** or **the web**) consists of documents that have been turned into web pages, which are stored on computers around the internet. These pages are interconnected by hypertext links. Each group of related pages in one location on the network is called a website. Information on any of these pages can be in any data format including text, graphics, tables, sounds and movie clips. Pages are written in the **HyperText Markup Language** (**HTML**). HTML is text with embedded codes (tags) that represent instructions for the display of the text and any images.

URL is an acronym for Uniform Resource Locator (pronounced YU-AHR-EHL). It is the address of a computer file or resource accessible on the internet. Sometimes you may find references to URI (Uniform Resource Identifier) or URN (Uniform Resource Name), which are the same as URLs.

URLs are a string of letters and punctuation in a set format. The URL contains the name of the protocol required to access the resource, a domain name that identifies a specific computer on the internet, and a hierarchical description of a file location on the computer.

On the web (which uses the Hypertext Transfer Protocol), examples of URLs are:

http://www.oshworld.com   http://www.ilo.org/cis
http://www.hse.gov.uk   http://www.cdc.gov/niosh/homepage.html

The last example shows a specific name of the resource (a file name in this case **homepage.html**) hence http://www.cdc.gov/niosh/homepage.html.

How to search effectively

Get the best results from your searches. The following instructions may help when searching for information on the internet.

1 **Clear searching**

   Develop a **clear understanding of what you need** from your information search. Be clear whether you are looking for general information or something very specific.

2 **Terms and keywords**

   When searching, think of:

   - related terms (both broader and narrower)
   - synonyms
   - other chemical names
   - legislation
   - differences in English and American terminology, for example boot/trunk.

3 **Search tips**

   Read the help or search tips when you are using any of the search engines listed below, because many people only look at the first ten 'hits' on any retrieved lists.

4 **Spelling**

   If you are unsure of the spelling think about possible variations, especially the different spellings found in American and English information, for example cheque/check.

5 **Boolean operators**

   Using what are known as Boolean operators – the words **AND**, **OR** and **NOT** – can help you get much closer to what you are seeking.

   Boolean logic operators are named after the mathematician

George Boole, who invented them. He used the operators AND, OR and NOT to express logical processes. More information about Boolean operations is given in the following section.

6 Authors

Do you know any author(s) working in this subject? By using the author's name, you may retrieve other references to similar work on the subject of your choice.

7 Institutions

Is there an institution or competent authority(ies) known to have done some work in this area? Again, try using the name and you may retrieve even more references.

8 Other sources

Do you know of any journals, indexing or abstracting service(s) specializing in the subject? Again you can add these to your search.

9 Information centre(s)

Do you know of any information centre(s) that specialize in the subject? This is similar to author searches because these information centres may well have produced a publication on the subject.

10 Other databases, databanks, CD-ROMs, floppy disks, either full text or bibliographic

Other databases may well be indexed, for instance other search engines, so if you cannot find information that you are seeking, look on another search engine or similar site which has lots of links. This will act as a 'hot link' for you to explore other material you may not otherwise have found. As an example, look at www.oshworld.com and under the country index, then click onto USA and go to US National Institute for Occupational Safety and Health, where you will find many sources of information.

11 Don't just stick to one search engine

Bookmark a variety and see what they come up with. Explore the ones listed below as part of your research and then decide which are the best to use for your work.

12 Search strategy

Work out a search strategy before starting your search. Many search engines offer ways of refining searches and these will save time and money in the long run. For example, decide:

- how far back in time the information is needed; you will save time by limiting your search
- which authoritative sites you wish to search
- what language to search in, for instance English only, which again will save time and money
- which words and phrases to use; remember to use English and the language of the site
- how to refine your search; most search engines offer two types of search – 'basic' and 'advanced' or 'refined'; in the 'basic' search, just enter a keyword without going through any additional options. Some search engines are so powerful that often you get good results with a minimum number of keywords.
- whether you want automatically to exclude common words. Most search engines ignore common words and characters such as 'where' and 'how', as well as certain single digits and single letters, because they tend to slow down the search without improving the results. Some search engines such as Google will indicate if a common word has been excluded by displaying details on the results page below the search box.
- whether a common word is essential to getting the results you want. If so, you can include it by putting a '+' sign in front of it' (be sure to include a space before the '+' sign). The one exception to this is 'the', which is so common it is not considered in searches.

The results may offer you the full text of the documents presented in different file formats. The documents could be in one of several formats, and will have the relevant indication, e.g. ergonomics.doc for a document in Microsoft Word software, or ergonomics.rtf if presented as a rich text file. The possible formats are:

- Adobe Acrobat PDF (.pdf)
- Adobe Postscript (.ps)
- Microsoft Word (.doc)
- Microsoft Excel (.xls)
- Microsoft PowerPoint (.ppt)
- Rich Text Format (.rtf).

When you are ready to start your searching, log onto the internet service provider (ISP) and you will be offered a 'box' in which you can key in your search. If you are looking for the Health and Safety Executive website enter:

www.hse.gov.uk

Remember then to press the Enter key on your key pad to activate the search. Some services may have the word GO immediately after the box; if so, click on it, again to activate the service.

13 Action if you cannot find a page

There may be a number of reasons why you cannot locate a 'home page' that you have used before. The page may have been removed completely, or had its name changed, or be temporarily unavailable. Try the following actions:

- Make sure you have typed in the home page correctly, in case you made a spelling mistake.
- If some specific page is suddenly not available, open the main home page and then look for the link because it may have been re-linked.
- If the above actions fail, go into one of the search engines, e.g. www.google.com, and look for the information again.

14 Newsgroups

Newsgroups make up Usenet, which can be thought of as the internet's distributed bulletin boards. They cover a wide range of subject matter. You can learn more about newsgroups at:

- www.learnthenet.com/english/html/26nwsgrp.htm
- http://computer.howstuffworks.com/newsgroup.htm/printable

You may need to contact your systems administrator or internet service provider to obtain access to these Usenet newsgroups. Alternatively, you can search newsgroup messages by using one of the following web-based search engines, which store and index Usenet newsgroup messages.

Tilenet   http://tile.net
Mailing lists   http://groups.google.com

15 Mailing lists

Mailing lists (run by list servers) are similar to newsgroups; the major difference is that new messages are sent to your mailbox directly. To locate lists that match your interests check:

JISCmail, www.jiscmail.ac.uk
UK higher education and research network

16 Internet search engines

There are a remarkable number of different search engines available across the internet; some of the most popular are:

AltaVista	www.altavista.com
Excite	www.excite.com
Go	www.go.com
Google	www.google.com
Google Groups	http://groups-beta.google.com/
Hotbot	www.hotbot.lycos.com
Ixquick	www.ixquick.com
UK Index	www.ukindex.co.uk
Yahoo!	www.yahoo.com
Yahoo! – UK and Ireland	www.uk.yahoo.com

Boolean logic operators

These operators were named after the mathematician George Boole, who invented them. He used the operators **AND, OR** and **NOT** to express logical processes, and Boolean logic represents a fundamental principle in searching information. It is the means by which terms used to describe a search topic are combined in a logical relationship.

You can use Boolean expressions to combine your search terms in a way that will give you more precise and relevant results than by carrying out a general search. Essentially, the AND operator and the NOT operator will limit your search results. The OR operator will increase the number of records you find.

The AND operator

Use the Boolean operator **AND** between two search items in your search when you wish to combine search terms and to narrow your search results. The AND operator requires that both search terms be in the same record. For example, the search statement Methane AND Mines retrieves just those records containing both methane and mines. Records containing only one of the terms are not retrieved.

The NOT operator

Use the Boolean operator **NOT** with a term in the main screen to limit your search by excluding records containing that term; for example, the search statement Mines NOT Methane retrieves records containing Mines but excludes those containing methane.

The NOT operator can be useful in eliminating false hits (occurrences of your term that do not satisfy your search request). But be careful . . . NOT should be used with caution since it can also eliminate relevant records, for instance Mines NOT Methane may also lose relevant records that discuss both mines and methane.

The OR operator

The **OR** operator can be used to broaden your search by letting you search for more than one term at a time. OR is particularly useful for searching synonymous terms.

If you want to find records containing information on a number of different chemicals, type them in and link them with the OR operator, for example Mercury OR Cadmium OR Benzene OR Ethylene. To carry out a comprehensive search, think of all the likely synonyms; type them in and link them with the OR operator, for example Visual display unit* OR VDU* OR Visual display terminal* VDT OR Cathode ray tube* OR CRT* or Display screen equipment or DSE. See below for an explanation of the use of asterisks in a search statement.

NEAR, FOLLOWED and ADJ operator

Not all search engines allow you to use 'proximity locators' such as NEAR and FOLLOWED BY. NEAR means that the keyword(s) you enter should be within a certain number of words of each other, for example confined spaces.

FOLLOWED BY means that one term MUST directly follow the other, for example visual display equipment.

ADJ for adjacent is exactly the same as FOLLOWED BY.

Relevancy rankings

Many of the search engines will give you results with a relevancy ranking. This means that the search engine has listed the 'hits' according to how close it thinks the search matches your enquiry. But a word of warning: the results may not be what you are really seeking. Some search engines are better than others; with experience you will find those that bring the best results in your subject area.

Truncation

Use of the asterisk, for example comp*, will find references containing words starting with comp, such as computer, computers and computing. Some search engines only search for exactly the words you enter in the search box and do not offer 'stem' or 'wildcard' word searching . If in doubt enter both singular and plural, e.g. 'airline' and 'airlines'. Read the 'hints and tips' information for each of the different search engines.

Sometimes databases and search engines use a different symbol such as the question mark ? to indicate 'truncation' or 'stemming', as this technique is known. If you get no results, or unusual results, try the asterisk and use the 'hints and tips' page. Some search engines, e.g. Google, will suggest corrections if you appear to have made a mistake in your search request.

Appendix 6
Library basics: filing, repairs, loans and reference services

We have included these notes because they can help people in a number of situations – those of you who are setting up a library entirely from scratch with no practical experience of library work, and those of you who are using this book as how-to training for your support staff.

The basic jobs that keep a library running are based on common sense, but they are easier if you know a few hints and wrinkles.

Filing

Libraries are traditionally divided into fiction and non-fiction sections, which works well in most situations. If you are setting up a college library to support the study of literature (where works of fiction will be study materials) you may want to read on to the section about filing non-fiction before you decide what to do. If you are setting up a workplace or other library that will hold non-fiction do not rush on to that section straight away: we are often surprised how many of these libraries have some shelves of fiction 'just to save people going to the public library at lunch time'. It's just as important that these shelves of donated materials or leisure reading are well organized and attractively presented as for the main business stock.

Fiction

Fiction used generally to be arranged by alphabetical order of the author's surname, either by the letters of the alphabet for small collections (Smith, Samuels and Saad would all be filed under 'S' and might be in any order depending on where there was a space) or in true alphabetical order for larger collections. True alphabetical order is not quite as straightforward as it sounds, leaving aside the fact that it can be quite complicated to get names in the proper order. Many libraries put all surnames starting with 'Mac' or 'Mc' in a separate sequence at the beginning of the letter 'M', as this avoids splitting a run of names where many people do not know the accurate spelling. Where there are a lot of authors with a common family name, you may want to use the first letter of the first name as an extra filing aid.

However, many libraries have now started to file fiction by broad type, so that crime novels are filed together, romances or historical novels in other places, and so on. This works well for small collections, too, and saves work in precise filing, but it can be difficult to allocate all the titles to categories (where do you put a historical romance?). So it is not quite as simple as might at first be thought to file fiction. The best system for you is the one that will suit your customers' needs best. If fiction is not the mainstay of your library, then you could simply file books on a shelf in order of the authors' family names.

Non-fiction

You have more choices with non-fiction. A classified order is best – that is, one where the books are arranged by order of subject rather than the names of the people who wrote them. Most people are familiar with the Dewey Decimal System, which arranges knowledge into ten broad categories. The system uses three-figure codes from 000 to 999 to indicate subjects, and – hence the name – it uses decimal places to subdivide complex subjects. It is possible to allocate very precise subject codes, although for a small service this is not really worthwhile. The broad categories are:

000–099: reference
100–199: philosophy
200–299: religion

300–399: social science
400–499: languages
500–599: science (pure science)
600–699: technology (applied science)
700–799: arts, sport and entertainment
800–899: literature
900–999: history and geography

These are broad categories so Dewey splits some related topics like books about languages and literature in those languages, and some groups like the 300 group have a lot of different topics in them. This is partly because the system is reflecting the state of knowledge in the late 19th century, when the emphasis on these categories was different. A team of editors keeps the system up to date by adding numbers for new subjects, but this is a bit like trying to keep pace with the demand for telephone numbers, and the codes get longer as time goes on.

The Dewey system is not the only system in use but it is the most universal and best understood. Academic libraries tend to favour the Library of Congress system, which combines letters and numbers to list subjects, while the Universal Decimal Classification (UDC) is used more often in specialist technical libraries, because it allows multiple subjects to be combined in a way that expresses their relationship to the main subject and shows the main emphasis of the book. Our reading list includes some potentially helpful titles, but if you have a professional librarian on your staff or can hire one, then he or she should bring these skills. If organizing the collection is important to you at the current stage of your information centre's development, ensure that you interview for cataloguing and classification skills when selecting temporary or permanent staff.

Reading list

Bowman, J. H. (2002) *Essential Cataloguing*, London, Facet Publishing.
Broughton, V. (2004) *Essential Classification*, London, Facet Publishing.
Kao, M. L. (2001) *Cataloging and Classification for Library Technicians*, New York, Haworth Press.
Mortimer, M. (2000) *Learn Dewey Decimal Classification (edition 21)*, Lanham MD, Scarecrow Press.

184 SETTING UP A LIBRARY AND INFORMATION SERVICE FROM SCRATCH

Repairs

Library and information centre materials sometimes get damaged, but in many cases can be simply repaired to a standard that will allow you to get more use out of them. The important thing is to ensure that any precious items – rare or expensive – are entrusted to a specialist as soon as any damage is apparent, so that you do not try to repair something whose value will be impaired or destroyed by a poor or bodged job. This leaves plenty of scope for enterprising library staff, however!

Guidance is available on the world wide web; some libraries have put their conservation manuals online, giving detailed instructions on a number of repair techniques. Jobs that are within your ability include: adding a plastic wrapper to protect the dust jacket; repairing small tears; replacing a page that has fallen out ('tipping in'); repairing damaged hinges and corners; and cleaning dirty covers. If more complex repairs are needed then you may need a more experienced librarian to advise you whether it is worth the cost of repairs.

If your collection is particularly valuable or if your information centre is located in a place that is vulnerable to water or other potentially damaging elements, it would be worthwhile considering a subscription to a disaster recovery service; the British Library website has links to several. See **www.bl.uk/services/npo/blueshield/freeze.html** as part of a site that connects to a number of library disaster plans.

Reading list

BonaDea, A. (1995) *Conservation Book Repair: a training manual*, Juneau, Alaska State Library, **www.library.state.ak.us/hist/conman.html**.
A Simple Book Repair Manual (1996) Hanover, New Hampshire, Dartmouth College Library, Preservation Services, **www.dartmouth. edu/~preserve/repair/html/introduction.htm**.

Loans

Most libraries lend stock to patrons, and you will probably wish to do so, too. You will also wish to get your stock back when your customers have finished with it, so you should set up and maintain a register of loans.

If you have decided to use any kind of automated system to operate your library it will almost certainly have a loans management element included. This will carry out a number of functions: it will link the item of stock with the borrower's name, and with the date the item is due for return (this is more use than the date it was borrowed, since many libraries allow different loan periods for different classes of borrower, e.g. lecturers, students, researchers); it will then issue reminders until the return of the item is registered on the system.

If you are going to use a manual system you will have to provide all of these functions for yourself. Begin by deciding how to register loans. If the library is open for long periods without a member of staff present, then even if you have an automated system you will need to devise a system of booking out borrowed items when the centre is unattended. One effective way is to mark up a solid A4 notebook as a register, with columns for the item details (author, title and shelf mark), and the name of the borrower and contact details. A final column is left to be ticked when the item is returned. If a horizontal line is drawn across the columns at the start of each day, and the date written below, then it becomes possible to see who has which item and when it was taken out.

You could also keep these details on cards for each day, or perhaps you would want to have a record for each book or each library user. If you have a small collection, this may be manageable but keep simplicity in mind and do not over-complicate the system. You will only really know if you have got it right the first time you need to find an item in a hurry for an important patron!

Your record of items lent could look like this if you keep it as a register, as shown in Table A6.1.

Table A6.1 Example of a loans register

Author	Title	Shelf mark	Borrowed by	Contact	Returned
Monday 1st August					
Smith, B	Economics	330	A. Jones	Ext 1234	
Brown, G	Science	500	K. Shah	Ext 3421	

The final column is ticked when the item is back in stock. After the standard loan period, perhaps three or four weeks, the library staff will examine the relevant day's loans to see what has not been returned. They will then contact the borrower either in person or using a pro forma note asking for the return of the item. This is followed two weeks later by a further reminder if the item is still outstanding, and after a third two-week period a decision is made about how to pursue the missing item or items. Some of the options that are commonly used are:

- to send a bill for the cost of a replacement copy – this usually gets the item returned, especially when it is an expensive report
- to stop the borrower from using the library until the item is returned – this can be difficult if the miscreant is a senior member of your community, and it could be seen as counter-productive to bar people when you want maximum use of the service, but it gets the point across
- to send a note to the offender's manager if you are in a workplace environment, drawing his or her attention to the problem and possibly asking for the cost to be refunded from departmental funds.

Fines are usually associated with public and academic libraries but if you have a problem getting items returned then you might choose to adopt them anyway. People are used to the concept of being penalized for failing to return communal property, so it may be effective to do this in the workplace too. You could regard it as partial repayment for the extra work that is involved in tracing and tracking missing items.

Reference services

In Appendix 2 we suggest some basic reference items for your information centre. People have become used to looking things up for themselves and we have referred more than once to the widespread belief that every usable item of information is available free of charge on the internet – when of course it is not. Make sure your reference collection contains what is needed for your clients. We provide you with details of basic items, but you will also have to identify the key reference items for your area of work; these will be specialist titles issued by professional bodies, or yearbooks produced by specialist publishers. Items in our reading list will help you to identify what you need – failing which, a visit to a good public reference library may be useful. Although some items have new editions annually, others are not published every year. This is just as well as some reference works cost over £100 per copy, and some libraries can no longer afford to replace every title every year. If a title is really essential to you, check with the publisher to see how often it comes out, and also whether it is available as part of an electronic package.

We recommend that you get to know the reference works in your collection or their online equivalents, so that you are confident in their use. Compare them to see how consistent they are; see how they can express the same information in different ways. Then if there is a need to provide a quick response to an important enquiry you can be confident that you are able to deliver accurately first time.

Index